I think many of us have been waiting for resou
deconstruction—but not resources that patron
asking big questions. Those anticipating such r   ir
library. Not only was I pleasantly surprised to r   to
its contents as a participant, I was encouraged as a follower of Jesus who has been dismissed
as somebody who refuses to be satisfied with simplistic answers. Ulmer has assured
me that I have a part to play and a responsibility to steward this skepticism with
faithfulness on behalf of fellow skeptics everywhere.

MARTY SOLOMON, author of *Asking Better Questions of the Bible*, creator and executive producer
of *The BEMA Podcast*

"Writing this book put me in some dangerous, irreverent territory." The opening line of
this book sums up the last several years of Preston Ulmer's life—and the lives of those
he interviewed for these pages. This book looks deconstruction fearlessly in the face; and
I tell you, at times, I could sense Jesus beside me, reading along, really listening to the
stories. Then, he opened his arms wide and beckoned to each person, "Come to me, all
you who are weary and burdened, and I will give you rest" (Matthew 11:28).

TRACI RHOADES, author of *Not All Who Wander (Spiritually) Are Lost* and *Shaky Ground*

As a pastor, I couldn't be more thankful for Preston Ulmer's voice in this critical and
essential discussion. In his new book, we come face-to-face with the reality that many
people in our culture are asking challenging questions, and simple or "churchy" answers
will not suffice. Through Preston's research and honest insight, we find hopeful inspiration
to discover Jesus, not religion. Whether you have questions about faith or know someone
who does, this book will bring you on a journey of learning grace and finding truth.

JEREMY DEWEERDT, senior pastor of City First Church

Brilliant! I couldn't put this book down. Preston is not only an incredible thought leader,
but he masterfully causes you to rethink everything you know about deconstructing your
faith. This is a must-read for every person who desires to gain clarity and understanding
while helping themselves and/or others through a process of biblical deconstruction amid
our constantly changing world and its challenges. Preston is spot-on; all you have to do is
follow the model set by the original deconstructionist, Jesus.

JIM WILKES, lead pastor of Journey Church

The body of Christ has been operated on by many inexperienced surgeons. And sadly,
there have been many forgotten scalpels, sponges, and clamps left inside, creating a body
that is less than whole. Preston is the delightfully uncomfortable surgeon who can help
repair the body of Christ. Whether we admit it or not, we all "deconstruct"—and many

of us do so in unhealthy ways. Thus, Preston offers us advice: "Deconstruction should be a means to an end; namely, the reconstruction of one's faith."

PETER HAAS, lead pastor of Substance, author of *Pharisectomy*

Preston Ulmer makes a bold and compelling case that the call to continually deconstruct and reconstruct our faith lies at the heart of what it means to follow Jesus. Just as importantly, Preston offers readers wise guidance on how to deconstruct their faith without thereby losing it altogether. I believe that *Deconstruct Faith, Discover Jesus* is as timely a book as it is important, and I enthusiastically recommend all thoughtful followers of Jesus read it and apply it to their lives.

GREG BOYD, senior pastor of Woodland Hills Church, author of Benefit of the Doubt

In *Deconstruct Faith, Discover Jesus*, Preston Ulmer methodically guides the reader through a process of reasoning, wrestling, and discovery. With sincerity and skill, he creates a conversation everyone should have. Regardless of where you are in your faith journey, I encourage you to read and digest this work.

GREG FORD, lead pastor of One Church

Preston is the best kind of conversation partner. Even when you don't agree with him, you can't wait to meet and talk again. His compelling love for Jesus invigorates your own, and you walk away seeing others, yourself, and God more like Jesus does. Written with compassion and veteran skill, this book allows us to step into the shoes of our friends and loved ones, to hear their pain and their hope. In the mirror of their doubts and questions, we see our own, and together we look to Jesus.

ZACK ESWINE, author of *Recovering Eden: The Gospel According to Ecclesiastes*

This book has two tremendous benefits: It provides a very helpful four-step method for undertaking the needed deconstruction of unhelpful teachings, doctrines, and versions of Christianity; and it winsomely invites readers to draw nearer to Jesus rather than run away.

REV. DR. DAVID P. GUSHEE, distinguished university professor of Christian ethics at Mercer University, chair in Christian social ethics at Vrije Universiteit Amsterdam

When we understand the incarnate mission of Jesus Christ, we will not distance ourselves from the curious, but we will position ourselves relationally centered among the skeptic, the critic, and the curious. Not only is this a book that I will refer to often; it's a book that I will give to those who are looking for Jesus—and those who want to help others see him!

DR. JEREMY JOHNSON, lead pastor of North Point Church

deconstruct
faith

How Questioning Your Religion Can Lead
You to a Healthy and Holy God

discover
Jesus

Preston Ulmer

A NavPress resource published in alliance
with Tyndale House Publishers

NavPress is the publishing ministry of The Navigators, an international Christian organization and leader in personal spiritual development. NavPress is committed to helping people grow spiritually and enjoy lives of meaning and hope through personal and group resources that are biblically rooted, culturally relevant, and highly practical.

For more information, visit NavPress.com.

Deconstruct Faith, Discover Jesus: How Questioning Your Religion Can Lead You to a Healthy and Holy God

Copyright © 2023 by Preston Ulmer. All rights reserved.

A NavPress resource published in alliance with Tyndale House Publishers.

NavPress and the NavPress logo are registered trademarks of NavPress, The Navigators, Colorado Springs, CO. *Tyndale* is a registered trademark of Tyndale House Publishers. Absence of ® in connection with marks of NavPress or other parties does not indicate an absence of registration of those marks.

The Team:
David Zimmerman, Publisher; Deborah Gonzalez, Acquisitions Editor; Elizabeth Schroll, Copy Editor; Olivia Eldredge, Operations Manager; Eva M. Winters, Designer

Cover illustration of line by Eva M. Winters. Copyright © Tyndale House Ministries. All rights reserved.

Cover illustration of star copyright © Flat_Enot/Adobe Stock. All rights reserved.

Interior illustration of limbic system copyright © corbacserdar/Adobe Stock. All rights reserved.

Interior illustration of brain silhouette copyright © picture-waterfall/Adobe Stock. All rights reserved.

Author photo taken by Meg White Photography, copyright © 2022. All rights reserved.

"Conversational Dashboard" image copyright © 2014 from *Conversational Intelligence: How Great Leaders Build Trust and Get Extraordinary Results* by Judith E. Glaser. Reproduced by permission of Taylor and Francis Group, LLC, a division of Informa plc.

The author is represented by the literary agency of WordServe Literary, www.wordserveliterary.com

All Scripture quotations, unless otherwise indicated, are taken from the Holy Bible, New International Version,® NIV.® Copyright © 1973, 1978, 1984, 2011 by Biblica, Inc.® Used by permission. All rights reserved worldwide. Scripture quotations marked ESV are from the ESV® Bible (The Holy Bible, English Standard Version®), copyright © 2001 by Crossway, a publishing ministry of Good News Publishers. Used by permission. All rights reserved. Scripture quotations marked MSG are taken from *The Message*, copyright © 1993, 2002, 2018 by Eugene H. Peterson. Used by permission of NavPress. All rights reserved. Represented by Tyndale House Publishers. Scripture quotations marked NLT are taken from the *Holy Bible*, New Living Translation, copyright © 1996, 2004, 2015 by Tyndale House Foundation. Used by permission of Tyndale House Publishers, Carol Stream, Illinois 60188. All rights reserved.

Some of the anecdotal illustrations in this book are true to life and are included with the permission of the persons involved. All other illustrations are composites of real situations, and any resemblance to people living or dead is purely coincidental.

For information about special discounts for bulk purchases, please contact Tyndale House Publishers at csresponse@tyndale.com, or call 1-800-323-9400.

ISBN 978-1-64158-604-7

Printed in the United States of America

29	28	27	26	25	24	23
7	6	5	4	3	2	1

For Piper and Brennan. This book is your reminder that I will always hold you tighter than tradition or religion.

Contents

A Note to the Reader

Dear Reader,

I wrote this book as an advocate for those who are calling for deconstructing faith in light of the damage certain religious traditions and perspectives have caused. I've sensed, seen, and suffered some of the injustices mentioned in these pages but not nearly to the degree of others. The interviews and research conducted quickly revealed that my background does not put me among those who are affected most by the spiritual abuse coming from faith communities. In fact, as a white, straight, middle-class American male, my words and thoughts will never fully capture the stories and wounds that many (perhaps even you) are feeling. It's also likely that my work as a pastor contributes to a mindset that will never fully allow me to see the man behind the curtain.

My hope is that I can use any influence or platform I have to steer people away from damaging practices that seem to be embedded in modern evangelicalism. It's an odd space to be in, but I'm committed to it because I'm committed to you! There is a world of hurt, fear, and manipulation within many expressions of faith that, for God's sake, must be torn down. May the words in this book calm storms that need to be calmed and start storms that need to be weathered.

Finally, to you, the reader, it is my heart's desire that "the fringe" be empowered once again. Not merely reached. Empowered. The stories in these pages represent a growing demographic that (in many cases) is devoted to the right things. Together, may we find a faith that looks like Jesus and settle for nothing less.

Preston

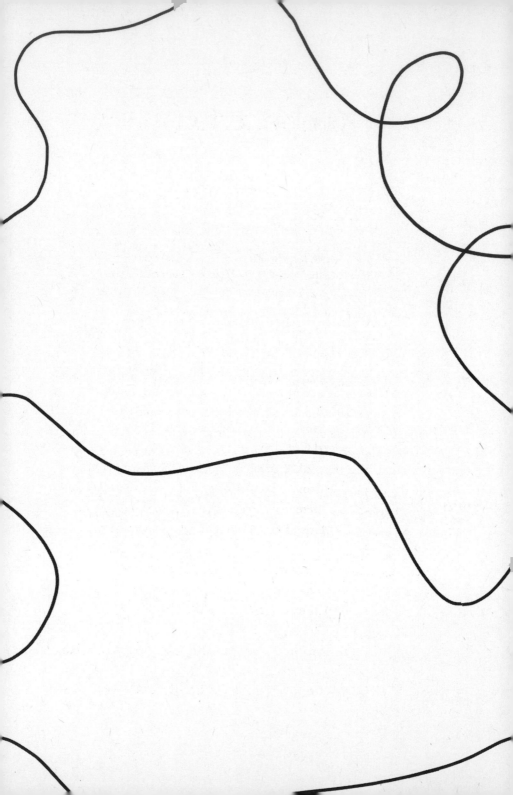

Introduction
Saving Deconstruction

*There is nothing so secular that it cannot be sacred, and that
is one of the deepest messages of the Incarnation.*
MADELEINE L'ENGLE, *WALKING ON WATER*

*Do not hope. Observe. Because when you do, you'll see how much
wonder the world actually has, and you won't be a cynic anymore.*
FLORA, IN THE MOVIE *FLORA & ULYSSES*

WRITING THIS BOOK put me in some dangerous, irreverent territory.

I was surprised to find Christ there.

Over countless hours of interviews and what sometimes felt like
unending interrogation from Christians and those who have deconverted from the faith, there was always a risk to this project. From
brothers and sisters in Christ, I would often hear remarks like

"How are you going to stay strong in your own faith?"
"Be careful not to become a skeptic."
"What if *their* questions make *you* become an atheist?"

I'm used to this from the work I do with the Doubters' Club.
Creating safe spaces for Christians and non-Christians to co-moderate
discussions isn't necessarily "playing it safe." But the warnings felt like
more than mere echoes.

1

These kinds of phone calls and text messages are all valid concerns from my evangelical friends. They didn't want to see me change sides from "that of the Crucified to that of the crucifiers," as New Testament scholar C. F. D. Moule put it.[1] I would hear a variety of sentiments from the unconvinced, as well.

> "You Christians need to experience the harsh reality of your
> hatred!"
> "So when did you decide you weren't a Christian?"
> "How the h*** can you work in the church world and think the
> way you do?"

Don't misunderstand. I wasn't going between these two camps for the sake of mining a good story for this book. Years ago, during my own deconstruction, I became desperate for an infrastructure that wouldn't become compromised during the storms of life. The theological home that I'd inherited wasn't my own, and I knew it had an issue with the foundation. It took time, but eventually I became convinced, and satisfied, by the story of Jesus' life. That is now the cornerstone of my views of God, Scripture, hell, politics, sexuality, and any other taboo topic (none of which have evangelicals cornered the market on). This project brought me all the way back to my foundation—the part of a home that no one notices unless it's crumbling. By no stretch of the imagination have I dismissed Christianity. On the contrary, I am convinced that Jesus deserves a better Christianity than what we're seeing in America and in the context of these heartbreaking stories.

If you look closely, you'll find that the way Jesus lived out his faith— deconstructing the parts of religion that humans had gotten wrong in order to express love for God and neighbors more authentically—is often overlooked, by Christians and non-Christians alike. In some ways, no-longer-Christians have gone beyond the No Trespassing signs into outright apostasy. Those landscapes will be evident to you as you read on. Not everyone who avoids the label "Christian" has left a Jesus-centric faith, however. Some of these people have a rather disorienting (but historically orthodox) approach to talking about their faith. It is unhinged from all dogmatic and abusive expressions of fundamentalism. They avoid the label because Christianity is too entwined with the former. They will never be evangelical again, but they are continually looking into the claims and actions of Jesus. One pastor I know who fits into this group classified himself as a "done." "I'm done with Christianity but totally in love with Jesus," he told me. And after hearing his story of abuse from his father, who was a deacon in their church, I don't think I'd call myself a Christian either. I've found that this group of "dones" is increasingly compassionate to the poor and marginalized. They thrive on uncertainty, mystery, and loving people well. In many cases, these people were trespassed on by men and women in power. They were told they weren't Christian *before* they chose to leave the faith.

Exiled before exiting.

Pushed out for wrestling.

Called "Trouble" for recognizing the tension.

And then given no attention since they were no longer attending.

I once heard a megachurch pastor say to church planters, "Don't worry about those who didn't come. Love those who did." Herein lies the uncomfortable truth for anyone who calls themselves a Christian: *God's attention will always be with those who aren't in attendance*—that's why he sent Jesus. God will always prioritize the unconvinced. He will always make way for the marginalized, and he will side with the skeptic when he can. Scripture reveals a very different God than the one so many people have walked away from. The God who calls us to reason together in Isaiah 1:18 knows that the heart has reasons that reason does not know. The heart needs the Incarnation to be convinced that it is truly known and truly loved. *That* is the peculiar God that we find in Jesus Christ. An incarnate Maker! Whoever told us that God is so holy that he can't be in the presence of sin was wrong. Precisely because God is holy, he must become like a sinner to win over the sinful. Theologian Dietrich Bonhoeffer reflected on this often. "God is not ashamed of the lowliness of human beings. God marches right in. He chooses people as his instruments and performs his wonders where one would least expect them. God is near to lowliness; he loves the lost, the neglected, the unseemly, the excluded, the weak and broken."[2]

If God's plan to reach those seemingly outside his grasp was the Incarnation, shouldn't all our attempts to reach the lost require the same? Not much can be done at arm's length, from the safety and security of the church. Neither can we expect that pastors and teachers must exceed any measure that we aren't willing to explore ourselves.

God knew that his best opportunity to populate heaven was by becoming one of us, by experiencing every dimension of what it means to be human. And so "this High Priest of ours understands our weaknesses, for he faced all of the same testings we do, yet he did not sin" (Hebrews 4:15, NLT). We don't need a personal, face-to-face encounter with Jesus to convince us of our belovedness. But Christ, without sin and coming into the world as a human, shows us that God loves us just as we are, not as we should be.

The Incarnation declares that God loves us, isn't scared of us, and wants us to be unafraid of him. So how do we declare these truths to the masters of suspicion of our day? The deconstructing, disoriented, disengaged skeptics.

We become like them, minus the skepticism.

If we learn to live through the eyes of our lost brothers and sisters, we become an ever more convincing group of people. And as soon as we start taking seriously the idea that God found the best option to be becoming one of us to get us, we'll start taking seriously the idea that, perhaps, we must do the same. Any group that we consider lost, misinformed, or even unreachable, God is inviting us to wear their shoes. Learn their language. Eat their food. We must not only know their names but also share their label. When it comes to the growing number of deconverting "nones" and "dones" in the West, we must get in touch with their reality. Know their weaknesses and temptations but encounter it all without deconverting. To do this, we must think like and encounter life like a deconstructionist. Scripture tells us that Jesus "did not sin," meaning Jesus has taken that which feels so secular and made it sacred. However sinful and secular deconversion feels to us, becoming a deconstructionist is its sacred, saving grace.

Rethinking Everything You Know for the Sake of the Unconvinced

This book is an invitation for the Christian who is desperate to be in relationship with their friends and family who are skeptical of Christianity. If that's you, I'm inviting you into the Incarnation for the sake of those who have not experienced how Christ would baptize a critical mind. And in the same way that the Incarnation was God declaring, once again, that men and women are sacred, we must remind the world that deconstructing is as well. How uninformed are those of us who follow the teachings of Jesus but not his incarnation.

One of the most pivotal books for me has been *The Body Keeps the Score*. I have learned more about the wholeness of my being (body, soul, and mind) from that book than from any of my thirty-plus seminary courses. The author, Bessel van der Kolk, offers a bold new paradigm for healing. There is a particular passage in this book that reminds all of us of how impactful it can be when someone chooses to walk in the shoes of another.

> At the opening session for a group of former Marines, the
> first man to speak flatly declared, "I do not want to talk about
> the war." I replied that the members could discuss anything
> they wanted. After half an hour of excruciating silence, one
> veteran finally started to talk about his helicopter crash. To

my amazement the rest immediately came to life, speaking
with great intensity about their traumatic experiences. All
of them returned the following week and the week after. In
the group they found resonance and meaning in what had
previously been only sensations of terror and emptiness. They
felt a renewed sense of the comradeship that had been so vital
to their war experience. They insisted that I had to be part of
their newfound unit and gave me a Marine captain's uniform
for my birthday.[3]

Van der Kolk continued this idea by talking about another time
when he counseled a group of veterans. His account of that story ends
with "For Christmas they gave me a 1940s GI-issue wristwatch. As had
been the case with my group of Marines, I could not be their doctor
unless they made me one of them."[4]

We must become like those we wish to help. In this case, renewing
your mind might include rethinking everything you thought you knew
for the sake of the unconvinced (Romans 12:2). As Shane Parrish is
believed to have said, "The best thinking is rethinking."

It's Not a Phase—It's a Holy Process

This book makes the case that in addition to being an invitation, deconstruction is a holy process that you can participate in with your non-
Christian family and friends. If you are a Christian, I assume you are
reading with one eyebrow raised, your head tilted to the side, and a list
of objections. I might as well tip my hand . . .

Deconstruction is a discipline of Jesus, and Jesus' followers would be
wise to reclaim it. That is this book's central, controversial idea.

Although much of this book is committed to surveying what exactly
deconstruction is and how it is helpful, there is a rather clear definition that
seems to capture the essence of the term. Deconstruction is "the taking apart

of an idea, practice, tradition, belief, or system into smaller components in order to examine their foundation, truthfulness, usefulness, and impact."[5]

This book is going to invite you into the mindset of a deconstructionist. A worldview that gives you a high capacity for paradoxes. A mental space that outweighs our self-interest in being right. A tendency to see Christian beliefs as inseparable from Christian ethics. Because what we believe about people does, in fact, determine how we treat them.

I originally set out to write a book that balanced deconstructing Christianity with reconstructing a generous orthodoxy that would be appealing to the doubting exvangelical. One that has Jesus' words and actions at its core. We will still go there. However, that's not our final destination. While I fully believe that getting to a Jesus-centered foundation should be the goal of deconstructing, I don't think it's about balancing the two. After conducting over sixty-five interviews for this book, I have come to learn that deconstruction is a discipline of the mind. A strategy for the thoughtful Jesus follower. Quite frankly, it's a way to stay Christian.

Deconstruction is like deweeding a flower bed. There are tools for it and ways to do it well. And it needs to be done constantly. Otherwise, the beauty of God is choked out by the nature of things.

My goal is not to tell you what you need to deconstruct but how to do it. I'm also not interested in telling anyone that they need to become a proud, elitist thinker. On the contrary! When we start to identify ourselves as anything other than a child of God, we stop becoming who God created us to be. Being a "deconstructionist" is no different. It's highly problematic when it has become our identifier. It's my hope that the inheritance of a sharp mind would be reclaimed by those who know there is more to Christianity than what we are currently experiencing.

For some, deconstructing the Christian faith is nothing more than an irreverent personal odyssey. For others, it's the only way they know how to be a Christian. If you don't land in one of those two camps, I'm certain you know someone who does. It's an unavoidable reality at this point. Everyone is talking about deconstruction, and it's here to stay.

Perhaps you consider deconstructing Christianity to be nothing more than a "phase of life." A time, somewhere in adolescence, when people ask questions about God.

Don't we all?

At which point you may be used to the church exposing doubters to apologetics. A few small-group lessons, maybe even a "How to Defend Your Faith" conference, and *poof!* Crisis averted. Last I checked, for the first time since 1940, church membership has dropped below 50 percent nationwide. Beyond the decline in church membership, there is an ever-increasing number of Americans who express no interest in religion.[6] This is a little more than a phase.

Perhaps you see deconstruction as a buzzword. Something that keeps popping up on the internet. It feels a lot like cryptocurrency. You know it's out there and that we should all learn about it, but it seems too complicated. Let's leave it up to the professionals. The only problem with that is the professionals are the ones deconstructing, and they are taking the masses with them. If you use buzzwords enough, they become normal.

I think we are there.

For many Christians, deconstruction isn't a phase or a buzzword but a habit. It's the modus operandi of their prayer life and Bible reading. It's the unavoidable tension between what someone *says* they believe and what they *actually believe* Jesus might be saying. Perhaps this is you. Deconstruction isn't a category—it's part of how you think. You are a deconstructionist. Your mind weighs everything. And as of late, everything about evangelical Christianity has been weighing on you. The good news is: You're in good company! The even better news?

You are in Jesus' company.

Jesus is our guide on this rather orthodox journey. My prayer is that you feel a sigh of relief throughout the pages of this book. Following Jesus is still the best way forward, and deconstruction is allowed. And once you have been comforted by the Deconstructing Savior, you can offer the strategy in these pages as solace to another.

This book is filled with people who are in the middle of processing their stories, and wherever they land, deconstruction and reconstruction are intricate parts of who they are becoming.

I should also let you know something that you may already be aware of: I will be processing on these pages as well.

It is because of my commitment to Christ that I must take all the stories and stats seriously. Also, I am trying to figure out how to pass this faith on to my own children. I have a vested interest in this topic because I want my children to know Truth better than I ever have. There are some devastating stories that I would rather my family avoid at all costs. So if this book feels more personal than academic, that's because it is. I will often cite the experts, but I'm not writing for them. This book is for the Christian who wants a more generous orthodoxy. One that allows, and expects, doubts from themselves and others.

In *The Anatomy of Deconversion*, author John Marriot states:

> Christians of all stripes must reflect on the kind of faith they are passing on to those they are ministering to. Is it a fragile and bloating house of cards comprising core tenets of the faith and our own micro traditions elevated to the level of orthodoxy that must be believed in order to be saved? . . . The irony is that the very means which some churches have used to keep their people within the fold significantly contributed to their deconversion.[7]

More important, it seems, than the stability of Christian doctrine is the ability to love like a true Christian. Which is the foundation of any doctrine we'd want to teach in the first place! Let this book be an attempt at loving the deconstructionist into a season of reconstruction and loving Jesus enough to follow him into that season ourselves, should he, in his infinite wisdom, invite us on that path.

I have a feeling that the Spirit is leading us all to deconstruct a faith that isn't working.

PART ONE

Why Deconstruct

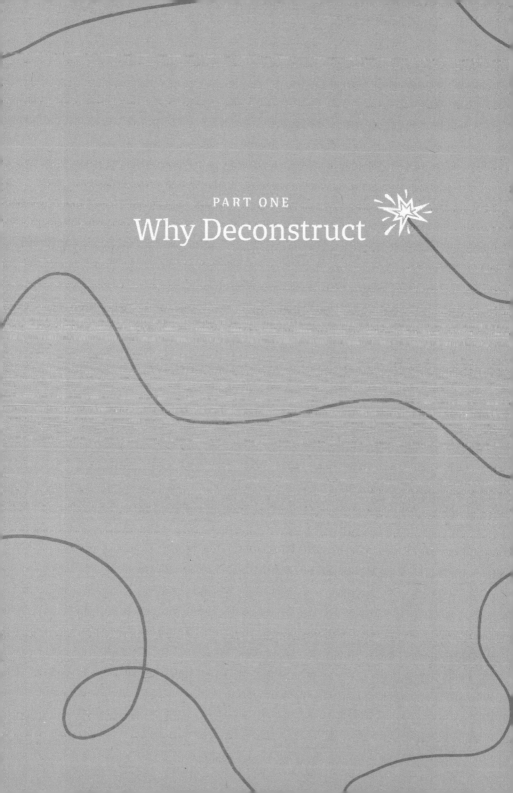

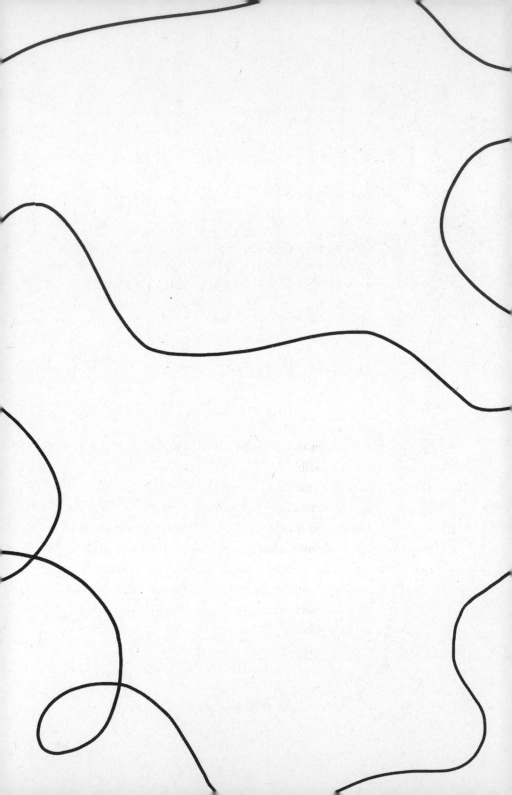

Chapter 1

Deconstruction Is Part of Our Spiritual Heritage

I have to remind myself that some birds aren't meant to be caged.
Their feathers are just too bright. And when they fly away, the part
of you that knows it was a sin to lock them up does rejoice.

RED (MORGAN FREEMAN), *THE SHAWSHANK REDEMPTION*

If you cannot get rid of the family skeleton, you may as well make it dance.

GEORGE BERNARD SHAW, *IMMATURITY*

ANYTIME I'M ASKED TO SPEAK on the topic of deconstruction, I try to do as much research as possible beforehand to figure out who will be in the crowd. It never deters me to know which brand of Christians will be listening; it just helps me anticipate objections that may arise. The frugality of our doctrines is usually exposed when talking about topics such as reforming Christianity, church hurt, spiritual abuse, and why we should listen to critics. Part of it might be because we don't want to believe such atrocities could have happened in the name of God. Another part could be that believing such things would mean admitting that we might have contributed to the problem. Either way, the sub-categories of deconstruction often seem like a taboo subject.

For this event, I was asked to give an hour-long speech on "Holy Deconstruction." It was taking place in Northern California, where one might reasonably assume people think outside of their biases—or so I thought. Sometimes even I make assumptions about the conservative or progressive perspective someone may have based on their location. I was speaking to a room full of pastors, however, and as Upton Sinclair puts it, "It is difficult to get a man to understand something, when his salary depends upon his not understanding it!"[1]

Flying in from the intemperate, noncoastal Midwest, I was surprised to see so many pastors in shorts or swim trunks filling the room. The room host read the brief topic summary that I had sent in weeks before, giving me enough time to turn off my phone and notice a coffee stain on my pants as I walked to the front. I talked for forty minutes about how a deconstructionist mindset can be (in its purest form) akin to the mindset of Christ. As soon as my talk ended and the Q and A began, a hand went up in the air from the front row, like a bullet in the chamber. I admire those who sit in the front row and are bold enough to ask questions.

"Thank you for being here," he began, cordially. The calm before the storm. "This whole topic of deconstruction reminds me of when the serpent asked Eve, 'Did God really say that?' Essentially, you're teaching people to question God's Word. It's the age-old sin! You're telling us that deconstructing our faith is a good thing? I have youth leaders who are doing this right now, and it's making them question the Bible. How am I supposed to help them deconstruct when it results in them asking questions about what I believe the Bible says?"

I was about to respond when I realized the interrogation wasn't over. The man continued, "Don't you think this deconstruction method is dangerous if it's going to result in these youth leaders seeing the Bible differently? How can they be on our church staff if we don't believe the same things?"

Finally, he asked a question that I will never forget: "What if teaching people to read the Bible through a Jesus lens makes us *all* change our minds about what the Bible says?"

Have you ever read such an honest, unfiltered question? Though I never fully resolved the impact of that question, I did let him know that clearly he understood the point of the lecture. Offering vacuous answers and quoting a few pertinent Scriptures isn't the answer. We must be willing to help people discover what Jesus has said about the issues they're wrestling with. Which means we must be willing to let go of our own interpretation of Scripture in the process.

You may be beginning this book with the same suspicion and concern as my front-row interrogator. If so, may I propose something new?

What if the ultimate tragedy isn't a lost person going to hell but a Christian who helps them get there by restraining the spirit of curiosity?

If you don't believe that Christ would endorse a process of holy deconstruction, then perhaps it would be helpful to see how the Christianity you hold rightly to is the result of the deconstructionists who have gone before you. The "cloud of witnesses" witnessed something entirely different from the religion of their day.

What if deconstructing religion is part of our spiritual heritage?

Overindulgent Christianity

When we deconstruct our religion or our faith, we aren't deconstructing what God said. We are deconstructing what *others say* God has said. The time we live in is historic! I don't mean it will be remembered in future generations (although that may be true). I mean we've been here before.

If you've ever studied the ingredients involved in former reformations, you'll notice that many of them sound like what we've heard about the deconstruction movement. See if any of these descriptions sound familiar:

Church leaders are afraid that people's own interpretations could lead them astray.

Challenges to doctrine are coming from those who have committed their lives to religion.

New resources and platforms have arisen to expedite the spread of
such news.
Religious leaders are shaming the voices who cry out for radical
reformation toward a Jesus-looking God.

If you are a Protestant reading this, this is the story of your ancestors,
not your enemies.
These are ancient echoes from centuries ago.
This is the sound of your spiritual migration.
Look back a mere five hundred years ago and we bump into a
character who radically adjusted the landscape of Christianity. Until the
1500s, religious leaders safeguarded their reading of the Bible to fuel
their finances, traditions, and power structures . . . until a random monk
decided to challenge everything. You may call him a reformer, but I like
to refer to Martin Luther as a deconstructionist.

Martin Luther as a Deconstructionist

From the sixth to the sixteenth century, Roman Catholicism was the
dominant form of Christianity. It's almost impossible to overemphasize
the scope of the church's power during the Middle Ages. The role of the
priest was emphasized at just about every turn. They baptized people at a
young age. They heard the confessions of congregants. They determined
the processes couples would go through to get married, and they offici-
ated the weddings. They were present bedside to provide last rights.
Other chores of the priesthood included distributing alms to the poor
and providing the educational services available. At the height of its
dominance, the church owned over one-third of the land in Europe,
which made it the most powerful economic and political force on the
continent. All this sounds like Roman Catholicism could be the foundation to the world's greatest act of charity, until you bring in power and
finances. During Martin Luther's day, these were gained by something

called indulgences, and they were the busiest and most lucrative undertaking of the priesthood.

An indulgence was a partial, or full, remission of one's sin based on the amount of money paid for forgiveness. Many times it would be accompanied with a promise to reduce one's sentence in purgatory. In other words, priests were acting as the gatekeepers of everyone's eternal state. I can't think of anything that I would give more money to than protecting the eternal state of my own soul. You may be wondering why people would put up with such an outlandish interpretation of Scripture. Confession booths and indulgences were based on the pope's interpretation of Scripture. Since the Bible wasn't yet translated into German or any other common language of the day, the religious powers could misuse spiritual authority without anyone knowing. They chose to line their pockets with the text, and unless you knew how to read Latin, you wouldn't know any better. That is, until Martin Luther learned to read Latin.

Luther was no stranger to the Roman Catholic hierarchy. Trained in the Holy Scriptures, he lived as a monk in multiple locations and constantly sought higher education. Receiving his doctorate from Wittenberg University was more than an academic achievement. This gave Luther a platform of authority just under the pope since the pope himself had to confirm the charter of the university. It was a symbol of confirmation upon Luther that his practices, and doctrine, were condoned by the priesthood and to be received by the people. All this was dependent on having total compliance from Luther. And why wouldn't he comply? He would be the main beneficiary of indulgences and receive many pardons from civil cases if he were ever in need of them.

The problem was Luther could now read the Bible and he had seen the belly of the beast. As it's believed he said, "You are not only responsible for what you say, but also for what you do not say." He could not sit back and quietly allow religion to be the face of God to the people. On October 31, 1517, Martin Luther nailed the Ninety-Five Theses to the front door of the Wittenberg Church. He wasn't trying to destroy the doctrines of his day. On the contrary! Luther was very specific. The Ninety-Five Theses were aimed at deconstructing the practice and theology of indulgences. Which, of course, challenged the whole system of religious gain. There were many educated deconstructionists before Luther, but Luther had something available to him that none of them had had: the printing press. Over eighteen hundred of Luther's writings appeared between 1517 and 1526.[2] Luther's ideas spread like wildfire to other priests and Catholics. In case you heard the Sunday-school version of Luther's story, his ideas were brash and radical. In 1519 he even called the pope the antichrist prophesied by Paul in 2 Thessalonians 2–3.[3] His most significant contribution, however, was translating the Bible into German. Luther was deeply convicted by the concept of a "priesthood of all believers," and he mobilized the idea by putting a Bible in the hands of anyone who was willing to read it.

Martin Luther was annoying to the religious ones with power.

He wanted the face of Jesus to be the face of forgiveness to the people.

By challenging the unbiblical practices of the Roman Catholic Church at the time, Luther split Christianity into two distinct camps— Catholic and Protestant. It's no accident that within the word *Protestant* is the word *protest*. It took a protest of religion to help people see Jesus. If you ever read Martin Luther's story in detail, you'll notice how the religious leaders did everything they could to discount his influence. During the rise of the reformation, Henry VIII condemned Luther and said that those who followed his teachings had no charity, were swollen with glory, had lost their reason, and burned with envy.[4]

If we aren't careful, we, too, will damn the deconstructionists of our day to preserve the destructive behaviors of our systems.

Prophetically Speaking

Luther might have only been following in the footsteps of the prophets. The prophets in the Old Testament were certainly reformers of their day. They were exceptionally gifted at reframing and reforming people's view of God. In fact, I believe Luther, Jesus, the prophets, and any other deconstructing reformers are primarily focused on God's relationship with his people. The rigorous attempt at deconstructing religion is always so that people will be mesmerized by the face of God and want to be in relationship with him.

Besides the "dense poetry and strange imagery," the prophets have a compelling quality about them. They are often crying out against the adultery and idolatry of the people and pleading that Israel return to God. According to the BibleProject, translating the prophets requires seeing some common patterns.[5]

> God rescued Israel from slavery in Egypt and invited them to become a nation of justice and generosity, that would represent his character to the nations. So this partnership required all Israelites give their trust and allegiance to their God alone.... But the leaders—the priests, the kings led Israel astray, and they broke the covenant. So this is where the prophets came in, to remind Israel of their role in the partnership. And they did this in three ways. First, they were constantly accusing Israel for violating the terms of the covenant. The charges usually include idolatry, alliances with other nations and their gods, and allowing injustice towards the poor.... Second, the prophets called the Israelites to repent.... That brings us to the third way the prophets emphasized the covenant: They announced the consequences for breaking it, which they called "the Day of the Lord."[6]

Notice how similar the prophets are to the protestors of the 1500s. And how similar the protestors of today are to the prophets.

Like the prophets, modern protesters of Christian culture are inviting evangelical leaders back to justice and generosity. Why? Because this represents the character of God to all nations! Additionally, the prophets faced most of their opposition from the priests and the kings who led Israel astray. It was the prophets' job to speak to those in power and bring a course correction to the nation of Israel. It was the prophets who used unvarnished language to bring attention to the broken covenant and misuse of spiritual practices. It was the prophets who let their entire life become an object lesson demonstrating the relationship between God and his people. Was this not why Hosea was told to stay married to a prostitute (Hosea 1:2)? Or why Isaiah walked around naked to illustrate the state of the nation without God's protection (Isaiah 20:2-4)? Or why Ezekiel had to eat a scroll (Ezekiel 3:1-3)?

The peculiarities of the prophets always deconstructed the way the Israelites viewed their current status before God. More times than not, it was to call out the divided allegiances Israel had with other nations and gods. In other words, Israel was sleeping with politicians and policies in order to gain something, while the poor were without justice or help.

This may sound graphic, but I encourage you to read Ezekiel 23:1-8 for context. The passage is full of imagery of God's people being like prostitutes who compromise their modesty for power. It's clear from the passage that Israel is lusting after the governors and commanders. At one point, God warns Israel through Ezekiel by saying, "There she lusted after her lovers . . ." (Ezekiel 23:20). The rest of that passage is so explicit, my publisher asked me to take it out. Go read it for yourself. The language of the prophets is unsanitized precisely to get the attention of the religious leaders. Sometimes, we are so far gone it takes offensive language to get us to see just how offensive our lives have become.

There is an alarming amount of language throughout the Bible aimed at religious strongholds. The prophets reveal to us a strange quality about deconstruction. Sure, it takes intensity and an all-in mentality. More than that, finding God through the chaos of a broken covenant will always mean offending the ones who broke the covenant.

I want to be careful to not equate all critics of Christianity with the prophets of the Old Testament. Of course the difference lies in someone's devotion to God. However, there is a prophetic liberty you are given if you deconstruct for the sake of revealing a more Jesus-looking God. The process will require approaching topics in their most real form. You'll have to see through the desperate eyes of someone who has been hurt and exiled. You'll create language that draws in the outsider and makes the insider uncomfortable.

Remember, deconstruction isn't destruction, but some people won't know the difference.

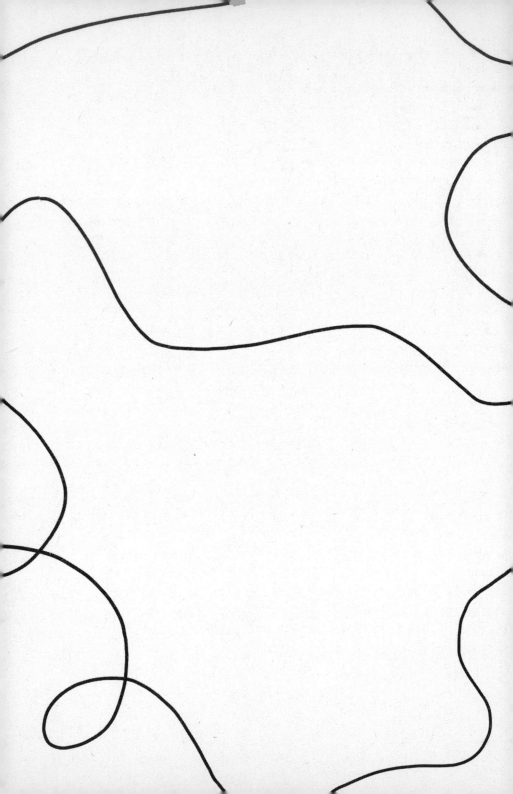

Chapter 2

More Questions Than Answers

In their effort to divorce language and experience,
deconstructionist critics remind me of middle-class parents
who do not allow their children to play in the street.

CHARLES SIMIC, *THE UNEMPLOYED FORTUNE-TELLER*

Taking on a challenge is a lot like riding a horse. If you're comfortable
while you're doing it, you're probably doing it wrong.

TED LASSO

HAVE YOU EVER HAD AN EXPERIENCE that punctures your theology and dares you to think differently? That's what happened to me when I visited Mount Rushmore.

Amid the breathtaking beauty in the Black Hills of South Dakota lies a mountain with four presidential faces in its side—George Washington, Thomas Jefferson, Theodore Roosevelt, and Abraham Lincoln. The overseer of the project selected these four presidents because he believed they represented four distinct trying time periods within America's history. From leading colonists in the American Revolution to stabilizing the nation into rapid economic growth, the presidents he selected were, for him, key figures of history. Men and women worked tirelessly through the Great Depression to blow up a mountain and transform it into something that looked entirely different.

Visiting this four-faced mountain was as far as we were going. My family was following my brother-in-law's family on their way from Denver to the Badlands. Both of our vehicles were filled with laughing and crying children, Cheeto-dusted fingertips, and frequently interrupted adult conversations. It was hardly the setting for a moment of wonder and awe. After the kids exited the vans, we navigated our way through strangers taking photos all the way up to the railing, which held back eager visitors from getting too close to the edge. And there it was—Mount Rushmore.

Stopping at Mount Rushmore, however dispensable it seemed, was infused with a sneaking, unexpected sacredness. I know it is a mountain, but it felt more like encountering a burning bush.

Later I learned that there is a dark side to the history of this monument. It saddens me that, although the vision was to create a wonder that the world would travel to South Dakota to see, Mount Rushmore was not a symbol of hope for the Lakota people, who owned the land.[1]

Thinking about Mount Rushmore brings up complicated feelings for those who know about its controversial history. I don't want to over-spiritualize the meaning behind the monument because even before its creation, the mountain was already sacred to the native people.

However, I did have an epiphany while I was standing there, gazing at the intricate faces that had been carved out of rock. My wife and I wondered, *How do people go about carving faces into the side of a mountain?* I can barely carve anything recognizable into a sandcastle! (Which, you have to admit, is harder than it looks.) Just how did they do it, and how long did it take?

The carving of Mount Rushmore took place from October 4, 1927, to October 31, 1941, and it involved the use of dynamite—lots of it. Around 90 percent of the carving was accomplished through dynamite. Afterward, to make sure you knew the difference between George Washington and Abraham Lincoln's faces, the workers used a process called "honeycombing." Honeycombing is where workers drill holes in close proximity to each other, allowing small pieces of rock to be removed by hand. In total, about 450,000 tons of rock were blasted off the mountainside.[2] That's roughly 900 million pounds!

Imagine that!

What I realized is that when something is as large and immovable as a mountain, the only way to transform it is by blowing it up. As I thought about this reality, it hit me:

Organized religion is like an immovable mountain.

It is large, hard as rock, and seemingly impossible to transform. So deconstructionists have realized that the only way to reshape their faith is by having their dynamite ready.

The time we live in is calling for something drastic.

This mountain of religion isn't meant to be climbed and conquered by a few. It's meant to be transformed into something that more closely resembles Jesus.

After committing his life to the mission of God, the apostle Paul didn't seem concerned about defending religion (read Galatians). It's arguable that he was a deconstructionist of his day, and his main objective was to bring the religious and the irreligious into authentic relationship with God, much like the work of the prophets who came before him. See, for example, this passage from Paul's second letter to the believers in Corinth:

> It started when God said, "Light up the darkness!" and our lives
> filled up with light as we saw and understood God in the face of
> Christ, all bright and beautiful.
> 2 CORINTHIANS 4:6, MSG

Did you catch that? Bright and beautiful.

Similar to the first daylight shot through darkness, the message of God is supposed to appear to the world as bright and beautiful. However you illustrate that text, the application is clear: The message of God should catch our attention. When the dust finally settles from the explosion, it is God we see.

When it comes to deconstructing our religion, we have to get the dynamite ready and light the fuse.

The goal is to reveal Jesus, not to preserve religion.

Something new is on the other side of the fearful statistics regarding the deconverted, the nones, and the dones.

The question we need to be asking ourselves is not *Why are people blowing up the faith we all know?* Instead, we need to be asking, *How can we make sure our faith looks more like Jesus when we're finished blowing it up?*

What Is Religion?

When I was a youth pastor, I showed "Why I Hate Religion, But Love Jesus," spoken word by Jefferson Bethke, to my youth group. It was at the service that we called "One Night," in which we told students to bring their non-Christian friends. Of course they were always welcome, but on this night, they were the guests of honor. The message was all about Jesus with a clear call to salvation, and the pizza was stuffed crust instead of simply hand tossed. We took no shortcuts! The whole night was geared at making a lasting impression. We had three types of Mountain Dew. One Night was wild.

My days as a youth pastor are long gone. Even back then, over a decade ago, I was fully aware that religion was an immovable mountain for the upcoming generation. In fact, when I showed the video of Bethke's spoken word, the youth erupted in affirming applause.

Especially when he said, "Jesus and religion are on opposite spectrums."[3]

It was the type of applause that only comes from shared experiences. What I was aware of then I am fully convinced of now. Cultural and personal narratives have the attention, and authority, when it comes to what people think about religion.

One thing I've discovered is that Christians who disagree about the topic of deconstruction are typically on different pages about the purpose of religion. It's no use having the same vocabulary if we are all using different dictionaries. Allow me to unpack this a bit.

It would be hard to dispute that religion, at its core, deals with both practices and beliefs. The practices of any religious group are an overflow of what its members believe. Not all beliefs practiced become a religion, but all religions have practices that flow out of what their adherents believe. But that is only what religion *looks like*, how we recognize it. Religion asks us to bow our heads when we pray. It makes allowances for confession. It ordains. Religion requires generosity and offerings. It takes people into questions of self. Religion handles disagreements with discipline or exile. It uses sacred texts for charity *and* power. The religious beliefs of any group determine their religious practice. We know it when we see it, yet we still have a hard time answering the question: What is religion?

Religion is not an easy term to define. It's a moving target depending on the baseline cultural narrative of the people using it. For skeptics, the overall impression of religion isn't a good one. In many cases, this is because our personal experiences with religion influence how we define it. This is often a point of contention with my Christian friends. "You can't redefine religion," some have told me. But the thing is: You can't properly define *any* metaphysical reality outside of culture and personal experience. Therefore, redeeming a proper definition of religion with a culture of people who have been hurt by it is a pointless endeavor.

The proper, academic definition of religion is a lot like underwear: It's good for support, but no one needs to see it. It's important that we don't focus on advocating for a proper, academic definition of the term. I'm not saying that defining terms accurately doesn't matter. But doing so will have limited impact when most people associate the term with their cultural narrative or personal experience. Definitions are only as useful as they are agreed on, and most people in the nonreligious crowd don't agree with, say, a list of comprehensive definitions.

Concepts that can't be weighed or measured rarely have an agreed-on definition. Consequently, we'll run ourselves down trying to defend a textbook definition of religion when other narratives are winning the day. We cannot answer the question *What is religion?* within the vacuum of seminaries and chapels. During one of my interviews, an exvangelical observed, "Perhaps you shouldn't ask 'What is religion?' Maybe you should ask 'What do you think about when I say the word *religion?*' instead." And when I framed the question that way, it became clear from the responses I got that for the deconstructionist, religion is like an immovable mountain. Or a gated community where only white evangelicals live (more on this later). One person said they think of lots and lots of bags. Baggage. Religion has something to do with baggage. All of us understand that.

I would argue for a hopeful definition, one that's historically rooted, oriented around charity and existential blessing. My soul is hungry and satisfied because of the vast scope of what "religion" has offered me. But the goal isn't to see God in the face of religion. Or to see religion how I see it. It is *to see God in the face of Christ.*

Many Christians will ask, "What about the Bible's definition of religion? Isn't the Bible still authoritative?"

I'm glad you asked.

If we must define religion, let's all settle for the most ecumenical, and historical, definition out there. A definition that clears the fog for those of us who get caught up in semantics. A clear statement about religion from the Bible itself.

The book of James seems to have been written before the Jerusalem Council (AD 50).[4] The council would be the first to decree that Gentiles were not bound to the Mosaic law. However, before the council, James sets a foundational definition for all those who would call themselves Jesus followers. James, the half-brother of Jesus, took care of the textbook definition of religion. As it turns out, religion isn't meant to stay in the text of any book.

> Anyone who sets himself up as "religious" by talking a good game is self-deceived. This kind of religion is hot air and only hot air. Real religion, the kind that passes muster before God the Father, is this: Reach out to the homeless and loveless in their plight, and guard against corruption from the godless world.
> JAMES 1:26-27, MSG

Another translation puts it this way: "Religion that is pure and undefiled before God the Father is this: to visit orphans and widows in their affliction, and to keep oneself unstained from the world" (ESV). Which makes me wonder what impure and defiled religion looks like. Perhaps it looks like the religion many people and cultures in the West have experienced.

Or, as Bethke put it in "Why I Hate Religion, But Love Jesus," "If religion is so great, why has it started so many wars? Why does it build huge churches, but fail to feed the poor?"[5]

People's lives don't change because we've redefined religion. People's lives change when the principles and practices of religion have refined us. At least for the time being, the church's history of abuse, cover-ups, and confusing doctrines has disqualified us from using a hopeful definition for the term. We are constrained to the definition of cultural patterns and personal stories. Religion was once a light for our path (Psalm 119:105), and now it's a mountain obstructing people's views of that same path.

It is the people who can't see a way forward who are being called deconstructionists.

What Is a Deconstructionist?

I had just landed after a two-hour flight to speak at a church that my friend Stewart planted.[6] The church was only a year old at the time.

By all main evangelical metrics of success, Stewart was killing it! Their annual income was three times that of the average year-old church. They had three Sunday-morning services. Which, also, was three times the Sunday-morning services of most year-old churches. And they had four people on staff—three more people than the average church their age. They had people, a building, a budget, and a lot of young adults. Young adults are some of my favorite people to talk with because they have a lot of questions about Christianity.

Stewart and I were just getting seated for sushi to debrief the Sunday service.

"Stewart, I'm working on a book about how Christians and deconstructionists have a lot in common and how both can help reform Christianity. I noticed a ton of young adults at the service. You must be dealing with some of the deconstructing I'm researching, right?"

Stewart chuckled, threw his hands in the air, and looked at his wife, as if she knew what he was going to say. Part of the church's success is because of his charismatic personality. Even our waiter took a step back as he prepared his answer. Stewart officially had the floor.

"When I think of deconstructionists, three things come to mind. One, they are emotional, argumentative, cynical people who want to burn things to the ground. Two, they tend to have a lot of church hurt and end up cannibalizing their own faith. And three . . . isn't *deconstruction* just a trendy word for what we all did in high school, question our faith?"

Like any good preacher, Stewart had three points to share. The only thing missing was a Bible verse, but those usually come Saturday night, after the sermon points are fully formed.

I don't agree with Stewart's assessment of deconstructionists, but I understand why he feels this way. Having someone deconstruct what we hold dear can be annoying. We start to feel exposed by their research, their questioning of what constitutes an authentic faith life, and even (quite honestly) their way of reading the Bible. Before we know it, a relationship with someone who is deconstructing can seem like a spiritual tug-of-war between who knows more and who cares more. It makes me think of what Os Guinness said in *Fool's Talk*, "Very few people are strictly and consistently logical, so to catch their small inconsistencies is merely to annoy them and put them off."[7] If we were to peel the layers back, we would quickly find that it's deeper than annoyance.

We feel threatened.

Even though most churches welcome questions about the faith, few of them welcome questions about the church's practices. Herein lies the threat to Stewart and many others, as well as the difference between what we "all did in high school." Deconstruction feels annoying to pastors because they, not God, are under interrogation.

Deconstruction as Art

There is a group of academicians who seem to always be taken seriously. These teachers don't come from Noah Webster's bloodline. When they define religion, they do so knowing that emotion is always attached to it. This group of scholars teaches us to find ourselves, and lose ourselves, all at the same time. They are artists, storytellers, and musicians.

Why am I writing about artists in a book about deconstructing faith? Simply put, artists reform the way we understand concepts that are outside of the realm of our senses. Historically, they have been a welcome authority within religion. Their authority remains, but they are now being labeled as "edgy," "irreverent," or "heretical." It's always uncomfortable when the Jesus Way seems heretical.

Artists

Artists are revered by us because they can paint (or otherwise visually depict) feelings. They show us what sad feels like. Or more, that it takes courage to be sad. They reassure us that we're courageous, even when we feel anything but. A paintbrush in the hands of a religious artist is quite a remarkable tool! It passes the logical, data-driven, "give me a definition" part of your brain and aims straight for the heart. *Isn't this how we feel about that?*, the artists ask. And even if we disagree, it's not without ample attention to the brilliance of what they've done.

The more thoughtful the artists, the better they are at helping us understand what we're trying to define. Some of their definitions are in small print as canvases in museums. Others, in a font size unknown to the modern computer, fill up museum walls. What is the Sistine Chapel if not how Michelangelo saw the relationship between God and man? Or what is *The Last Supper* if not Leonardo's attempt to show us the face of God in the presence of betrayal? Which is, in fact, the story of God and mankind.

Storytellers and Musicians

Artists aren't experts, just authorities. Storytellers and musicians fall into this same category. Their words and melodies paint pictures for the heart to see.

Storytellers have always had a place in society. My Irish friend, Andrew, is one of the best storytellers I know. Granted, he usually tells stories from the pulpit, but he would captivate an audience in any setting. I never look at my watch when Andrew is speaking. My imagination is too preoccupied with the picture he is painting. As we all know, good stories are told to make us think.

Andrew has explained to me how storytelling works in the Celtic culture. In this tradition, storytellers were referred to as *anam carras*—soul friends. They used to tell stories to guide the spiritual journey of the hearer. Anam carras functioned as guardrails on the freeway of life. Jesus was drenched with the spirit of an anam carra every time he told parables. He was *the* authority on the topic of religion, yet he chose to steer the heart and mind through storytelling.

Unfortunately, in our attempt to define religion with dogmatism and doctrine, we have forsaken the importance of how the Ultimate Storyteller defined it. Jesus could just as easily have transcribed "This is religion . . ." on stone and left it up to his followers to never add a jot or tittle. Instead, he told stories. Stories that would move his listeners—some of them to follow him, others to crucify him. But move them nonetheless. Jesus had an uncanny ability to contrast those attempting to live by the *letter* of the law with those trying to live by the *spirit* of the law.

Jesus wasn't concerned about defining religion and labeling deconstructionists (probably because he was one). He was concerned that those who call themselves religious were becoming increasingly Christlike. That was the main idea for most of his stories. How to treat the people around you as God would have you treat them. In his book *Jesus the Storyteller*, Stephen Wright points out some peculiar tendencies we Jesus followers have when it comes to understanding the heart of religion. In our quest for more information about God, we end up reducing him to statements and principles. Words that we can project onto those who don't live according to the law, instead of stories that we tell one another for personal, and communal, transformation.

The stories Jesus told, and Jesus' activity as a storyteller, have been strange and usually unintended casualties of the modern quest for the historical Jesus. Repeatedly, this element of his life has been marginalized, and the stories themselves have been, in effect, transposed to other rhetorical forms, sometimes in the effort to establish criteria for distinguishing the Evangelists' implied interpretation of the stories within the Gospels from the force they would have carried for Jesus and his hearers.[8]

More recently, I've noticed the spirit of an artist in graphic designers, muralists, and taggers (graffiti artists). Caught up in the hurry of personal opinions and an exhausted life, we scroll and stroll past them. They are on our newsfeeds and in our peripherals. They are declaring definitions from a deep, soulful place. Even graffiti has a way of making spray paint sacred.

Holy Taggers

My oldest daughter, Piper, was talking with me about the terms *legal* and *illegal*. Okay, I'll admit . . . this is one of those times where you need to be very clear with defining terms. It's always better to have this conversation with your child before a judge has to.

"Dad, is spray-painting a train or a house legal or illegal?" She asked me from the backseat. Her question immediately made me nervous. It landed somewhere between "How was your day?" and "Where do babies come from?"

"Yes," I told her. "It's called vandalism, and vandalism is illegal. You have to get permission to spray-paint someone's property."

Just then, we slowed down for a train to pass. The majority of it was covered in graffiti. Piper spoke up with a frustrated curiosity: "You're telling me that those beautiful words and pictures are illegal?"

Grateful the train was moving too fast to read all the graffitied words, I told her that she was right. "It takes skill to spray-paint," I said, "and it seems like the taggers are trying to tell us something." I looked in the rearview mirror to see her expression. She still wasn't having it. She was staring out her window. You know, the way you stare when you don't want to talk because you know you are being misunderstood.

"Piper, the one thing they are missing is permission. If they have permission, it's legal."

"Like murals on a building?" she exclaimed. Finally, a loophole to the rules! Lord, help us.

"Yes! Murals are legal because the owner has given the artists permission."

"Okay, how about this . . ." Piper was now trying to rewrite the law. As I'm writing, I'm realizing that I'll be too busy during her teenage years to write a book. So enjoy these stories while you can.

Piper continued with her reasoning: "How about graffiti is only illegal if it's ugly. And all of us get to decide what's ugly. I think that train looks better with graffiti. Otherwise, it's just a train. Or a building. Or a house. The spray paint gives me something to think about. It makes it more than just a train. You have to be an artist to spray-paint like that!"

I interviewed the graffiti artist Leighton Autrey for this book. Leighton has been commissioned to do murals at major-league baseball stadiums and million-dollar fundraisers, and he's made custom pieces for private collectors. All with a spray can. He's a long-time friend of mine. A fellow Christian whose journey is marked by deconstructing, and reconstructing, a faith that looks like Jesus.

"My art isn't meant to help the religious become more religious. It's meant to help the non-Christian think differently about God." He started laughing before giving me his next line. "It's happened numerous times when someone will be staring at a piece of my art and say, 'This piece is unreal! What is it?' I'll reply with something like, 'It's showing you the destruction of the Egyptians. It's from the Bible.'"

"What do they say to that?" I asked.

Leighton said the normal response is "What? That's giving me a whole new perspective on the Bible." Many times, these conversations encourage non-Christians to learn more about God. Leighton shared about a time he led someone to Jesus at 3:00 a.m. at a bar in Detroit, all from a discussion of his artwork.

"What about more religious folk?" I asked him. "How have they responded to your graffiti art?"

"It's really a mixed bag. When I started painting, I had quite a bit of feedback that my artwork 'isn't Christian.' It's not safe. It's intense. But it hit me that I'm doing exactly what I'm supposed to do. I'm getting people's attention. I'm helping Christians deconstruct their Christianity and non-Christians think about God. I'm not making graffiti art just for Christians. I do this for everyone."

Leighton showed me that some deconstructionists use a spray can as dynamite.

Artists deconstruct religion for us. It feels illegal to the highly religious. But artists don't get their permission from the religious. Their permission comes from the masses that they themselves are part of. Vandalism is to the train what deconstruction is to religion. Sure, it feels illegal. But that's only because the people in power haven't given permission. The time of waiting for permission to deconstruct is over. Artists are speaking all around us. These words attributed to Roman poet Horace say it well: "A picture is a poem without words." We need not dismiss art so quickly. If there is any authority on the topic of deconstruction outside of what you may already think, it lies with the artists, storytellers, and musicians. Are you listening to them?

Take a moment to slow down and listen with your heart. Many artists are speaking to the existential questions of the soul.

Who am I?

Why am I here?

What is the most right thing to do?

What is God like?

How should we handle suffering?

What comes after this life?

These questions are religious, and artists, storytellers, and musicians are evaluating them in light of what is useful and true. Artists aren't professionals at defining things, but neither are any of us. Even the cleverest wordsmith will experience more reality from a piece of art than a well-thought-through definition.

"The Journey I Most Feared..."

Priest and world-renowned author Henri Nouwen had an unplanned encounter with a copy of Rembrandt's painting *The Prodigal Son*. Hours of staring at this image changed how Nouwen defined religion and the purpose of his existence.

Prior to this encounter, Nouwen had taught at the University of Notre Dame, Yale Divinity School, and Harvard Divinity School. He had authored thirty-nine books on the spiritual life. Scholar and wordsmith is an understatement. Nouwen's brain was a library of undocumented thoughts, and his spirit never slept. Yet one sitting of meditating at the feet of Rembrandt's painting deconstructed what Nouwen thought he knew, how he saw his role in God's story, and where he would spend the rest of his life. He referred to this moment as "the journey [he] most feared" because he "knew that God was a jealous lover who wanted every part of [him] all the time." And Nouwen wondered, "When would I be ready to accept that kind of love?"[9] Nouwen wrote a book on this experience titled *The Return of the Prodigal Son*. The book is well worth the read. In it, Nouwen writes of the revelation he had as he slowed down to consider Rembrandt's piece:

> All of these mental games reveal to me the fragility of my faith that I am the Beloved One on whom God's favor rests. I am so afraid of being disliked, blamed, put aside, passed over, ignored, persecuted, and killed, that I am constantly developing strategies to defend myself and thereby assure myself of the love I think I need and deserve. And in so doing I move far away from my father's home and choose to dwell in a "distant country."[10]

Cannibalizing Christianity

Anyone who has built their lives, and livelihood, around the certainty of evangelical claims will be threatened by someone who is deconstructing mainstream evangelical religion. So the two opposing options become

1. Don't build your life around the certainty of evangelical claims; or
2. Don't practice deconstruction.

Many Christians today tend to think, *How could we possibly choose option one? If we don't build our lives around the certainty of Christianity, then what is the purpose of faith?*

Following this logic, it seems the better option is to reject the practice of deconstruction and regard it as dangerous.

But when we think this way, people get hurt, as our track record shows.

Less than one hundred years ago, during the rise of the civil rights movement, Jim Crow laws were being established in the name of religion. This came, of course, after white Northerners and Southerners would gather, Bible in hand, to maintain segregated communities. The proslavery ideologies of that day were enforced through the misreading of Scriptures like Genesis 9:24-27. Segregationists used this passage, referring to the "supposed 'curse of Ham' as proof that God had made 'Negroes' to be slaves." Further, "They thundered that abolitionists were distorting the Bible and threatening the Christian social order of the South. Such extremists, they argued, had no right to impose their own distorted and dangerous orthodoxy on everyone else."[11] The segregationist's folk theology that ruled that day did so under one dangerous assumption: Don't deconstruct Christianity. Segregationists believed that *their* interpretation of Scripture was *the* interpretation of Scripture. *God created the races separately*, they would tell themselves, *and he did not intend for them to mix.*

From the fourth century forward, various philosophical and ideological systems influenced Christianity. And when an ideology of the world influences Christianity, it manifests itself by Christians emphasizing the centrality of something other than Christ, protecting that emphasis by twisting Scriptures and exiling those who differ. From Platonism and Alexandrian philosophies in the early church to Locke's liberalism and Marx's communism in the reformed to Enlightenment years. From Nazism to evangelicalism. We are kidding ourselves if we think that we have arrived at the proper interpretation of Scripture on every passage that has something to say about the issues of the day. God help us if we repent of the actions of our past without changing our minds in the present.

Is it even repentance at that point?

Telling the Truth Changes Things

Telling the truth is good for everyone except for the institution that thrives off misinformation. A true deconstructionist isn't trying to disprove Christianity but to improve it!

I have a soft spot for documentary films. If I had a day off from work and had the chance to watch either a movie or a documentary, I'd pick the documentary. Don't get me wrong—I love movies, but documentaries have a way of challenging my mind.

Documentaries spark conversations, while movies already have them scripted.

Documentaries tell the story of real life, while movies help us escape it.

Documentaries challenge common assumptions, while movies protect them.

Deconstructionists are a lot like documentarians.

In 2013, my oldest daughter was but a baby, and staying in a hotel with her was a challenge. She was at that age when getting her to fall asleep in the same hotel room as us should have required a master class. She needed clean diapers. Blankets under the sheet covering the crib mattress. The air at just the right temperature. No light whatsoever creeping in through the curtains. And no sounds other than the white noise coming from the out-of-date tablet that served no other purpose than being a sound machine. After all these requirements were attended to, Lisa and I snuck into the bathroom to watch our first documentary on Netflix together, *Blackfish*. Sharing a single set of headphones, I might add.

At that point in my life, I had never seen a more compelling documentary! This one was about SeaWorld's inhumane treatment of their animals, primarily their killer whales. That documentary changed the way I viewed SeaWorld.

Like my wife and I, many people enjoy Netflix documentaries. According to Insider, at least 73 percent of Netflix viewers watched one documentary. That's over sixty-eight million people![12] Netflix's vice president of original documentaries, Lisa Nishimura, told the *New York Times*: "What we've discovered is that we can elevate storytelling and bring it to a global platform and create a cultural moment."[13] In the case of *Blackfish*, it was a great moment for the uninformed and unconvinced—and a terrible one for SeaWorld.

Blackfish isn't just about how badly SeaWorld treats their orcas; it is also about how well orcas need to be treated. I have learned to not despise the deconstructing mind. We must allow its light to shine into the dark recesses of church history and illuminate the injustices committed in the name of God. We must let deconstructionists apply pressure to the wounds of current evangelical practices to help stop the bleeding. We must understand that the untamed energy of these sacred documentarians needs to be channeled through the people of God. We must learn how to participate in the renewal of all things by deconstructing the ideas, beliefs, and practices that are not part of God's forever plan. At the heart of it all, we must become specialists in this area because Jesus was a deconstructionist.

And he refused to settle for anything less than the love of God.

Chapter 3

Deconstruction versus Deconversion

There is a crack, a crack in everything. That's how the light gets in.

LEONARD COHEN, "ANTHEM"

Don't criticize what you don't understand, son.
You never walked in that man's shoes.

ELVIS

"ANOTHER HEADLINE about a former pastor who has completely deconstructed his faith, Lisa. What is going on?"

We were driving the kids to get ice cream, and I couldn't process quietly anymore. My wife knew this question had an underlying irritation to it. I was asking as a former deconstructionist. Someone who was undone by questions, and I still have the spiritual fatigue to prove it. This kind of news continues to take the wind out of my sails.

"Who? What happened to them?" She responded in a whisper. The kids quieted down. I think they could tell I was upset. Cue the latest Justin Bieber single! Once the kids started singing along, we kept talking.

"Joshua Harris decided he is no longer a Christian. Someone who was almost single-handedly responsible for the guilt-ridden altar times of every youth camp I attended. He pastored and wrote books . . . Now, his new mission is helping people deconstruct their faith." I was visibly upset.

Lisa waited longer than normal to respond. It made me uncomfortable, so I turned up the music. I'm a seven on the Enneagram, so I tend to avoid pain at all costs. The music wasn't loud enough, evidently, because I regularly hear the echoes of her response.

"Preston, do you think you will ever leave Christianity?" Lisa saw straight through my angry facade.

I was judging Joshua Harris, and all those before him, because deep down they reminded me of my own struggle. Their public deconstruction of Christianity reminded me that I'm never as certain as I want to be.

"Huh," I replied. "I don't think so. What makes you ask?"

"I've noticed you get fixated on these stories. They really seem to affect you. You have a hard time shaking them."

She was right. I understood what Jacques Derrida meant when he wrote, "I always dream of a pen that would be a syringe."[1] I was a user. These headlines were my drug.

By the time we got to Andy's Frozen Custard that night, I realized that my anger about the situation was more about my insecurities than it was about anyone else. With every deconversion story, I was reminded that deconversion is a possibility for all of us who make an idol out of certainty. Additionally, it occurred to me why I get single-minded about deconstruction stories: I am attracted to the radical candor, and spiritual courage, that it takes to ask questions around the truthfulness and usefulness of Christianity.

Perhaps you have felt the same thing.

The need to interrogate some of our own claims.

It's the unnerving reality that we have outgrown the certainty of our youth, and we feel more at home with questions than we do answers. Questions like

Why is it wrong to be gay, but you can shoot someone for trespassing on your property?

How come every pastor acts like they know what the Bible says, but everyone seems to be saying something different?

Lately, I've been wondering how a prayer gets you into heaven, but a life of loving people well, without faith in Jesus, still lands you in hell. That one has been bothering me for a while.

Instead of realizing that deconstruction is a normal part of the journey for Christian pastors and mystics alike, we bury this season of spiritual development so no one can see.

Like a beach ball that you're trying to hold underwater.

Consequently, sitting in the pews and watching online are a bunch of closet deconstructionists who don't feel accepted or understood in church. Stuck in the tension between authenticity and apostasy. Tempted to be swept away by the rising tide of #exvangelicals. Tilting their heads in curiosity every time a new headline pops up about a former Christian superstar who has now, for all intents and purposes, fallen from the heavens. It's not that we want that to be our story. It's just that we wonder if there is another way forward without abandoning Christianity entirely.

When the answers aren't working, people move to questions. And when the questions aren't allowed, they feel like they don't have a home anymore. It's in those times of being completely disoriented by the church's reaction to our journey that deconstructionists welcome us in. I'm not the only one who is intrigued with these stories.

You keep rereading the headlines too.

Forget the headlines! What we need are the confessions of Christians, and former Christians, to help shed light on the rubble before we rebuild. People like Josh help us see what we are both unable and unwilling to see. If God is the essence of good, then we need people to point out where we have gone bad.

Meet Joshua Harris

If you grew up in the evangelical culture sometime in the last twenty years, you have probably heard of the book *I Kissed Dating Goodbye*. That was Josh's debut, *New York Times* bestseller. Written when he was twenty-one years old, no less! He did write many books after that, but none of them had the searing effect of his first. Josh's book was a fortress for the morally upright and the virgins. I remember reading it in high school and telling my youth pastor how much I wanted to honor God through living like this book told me to. Knowing that I had a girlfriend at the time, my youth pastor reassured me that courting was better than dating. "This means the two of you can't kiss," he told me. I was asking for forgiveness at the altar by the next Wednesday.

I've been familiar with Joshua Harris as a fan, a skeptic, and a spectator. Just minutes into our interview, it felt like he was an old friend. His demeanor was unassuming. He smiled a lot. And a lamp behind his head gave the appearance that Joshua Harris had a halo. It was quite pleasant! Josh was not who Christians said he was. Headlines painted him to be an apostate who has given up on spiritual matters. After our conversation, I'm convinced that Josh is still on a journey—as we all are. And that deconstruction is not a phase or a season; it's a mindset. An attempt to authentically match up what we believe with how we behave, and to measure it all against its helpfulness in the world. This is at least the case with Josh.

"I've never wanted to be part of something that gets people to believe differently or walk away from the faith," he told me. "I just love it when there are people who are saying, 'Let's dialogue, let's interact with people who think differently, let's be open to conversation . . . and let's be open to being convinced.'

"Even with *I Kissed Dating Goodbye*. There are a lot of things about that book that I am regretful of and have apologized for," Josh explained. "It was a sincere attempt to live out convictions about love and sexuality . . . to bring into alignment belief and life."

As Josh talked, he kept looking in different directions, as if he were watching different episodes of his life playing out. Then he looked back at me and said, "I feel like *journey* is a great word. It's overused, but a great description. I'm still on a journey. I'm still learning and growing."

We discussed how he's been labeled a deconstructionist. It was never an identity that Josh was striving for, but he believes people started associating him with that crowd because of the drastic announcement he made about losing his faith. Josh then said something that made me realize I was talking to someone with massive intellectual integrity. Reflecting on his public deconversion, he shared:

> When I realized internally that I wasn't believing the same way, and I wasn't having those same convictions, it grated on my soul to be living under the benefits of that [Christianity] when it wasn't actually the reality. I think I have such a respect for Christianity . . . if it's real, it needs to be taken seriously and not just played around with

Josh's public renunciation of faith was largely due to the pressure he felt as a public persona. While he was questioning, he didn't want the benefit of his books and speaking engagements to make him come across as a certain brand of Christian, hindering him from authentically searching for truth.

When Deconstruction Leads to Deconversion

In our interview, Joshua Harris gave some helpful clues for why deconstruction sometimes results in deconversion. These are important for us to know so that we can avoid deconversion as we deconstruct and teach others to do the same.

An Elitist Mindset

Within mainstream evangelical Christianity, an elitist mindset isn't uncommon. It perpetuates judgment toward people outside the faith, as well as those within it. Elitists think that those who aren't as theologically precise as them are, at best, compromising their faith and, at worst, enemies of the faith. As we discussed this mindset, Josh confessed how inflexible he'd once been with his own faith. "Everything was a hill to die on," he told me. "I was always looking over my shoulder to make sure I had things right. And ultimately, it was exhausting."

People have used the Bible to support an array of ideas throughout history. From erecting hospitals to launching the Crusades. From helping the poor to chasing prosperity for themselves. In any era of Christianity, where you find a strong agenda, you find an unwavering leader with an inflexibility to their faith that stifles spiritual growth in themselves and others. Except for Jesus, that is. Jesus is the only leader I know of who was intentionally ambiguous in his answers to questions that didn't have an eternal impact. He wasn't wishy-washy in his beliefs; he just didn't want people to be so caught up in focusing on the wrong things that they missed out on the most important thing of all: life with him. Two things that Jesus never wavered on were loving God and loving people.

As Christians, we want to love God and other people, but as humans, we often struggle with doing this well in our day-to-day lives, as is evident in our interactions with believers and nonbelievers alike. Gaia is an atheist who deconverted from Catholicism. When we were talking, I asked her what her vision for the church would be moving forward. "I would want to see [members] love their neighbors, love the LGBTQ+ community . . . just love people better. You Christians are in for a brutal wake-up call when it comes to the aftermath of how you have loved one another."

I waited before responding because I didn't want to get defensive. "Gaia," I said, "what you just described is the way of Jesus. I agree. We Christians must get back to the way of Jesus."

It is impossible to lean into the brokenness of the human condition when we are preoccupied with being right. A single mother doesn't need to be told that she should have waited until she was married to get pregnant. She needs help with paying the bills, raising her child, and going back to school. Someone on welfare doesn't need to be told they're lazy but needs food and shelter and skills training or help filling out disability paperwork. If we think we have to prove we're right in every situation, we'll end up proving how wrong Christianity is. An inflexible, rigid theology that plays to our biases and preferences is an ingredient for deconversion.

Becoming an Early Advocate for a Specific Brand of Christianity

Harris's second confession was about becoming an early advocate for a certain brand of Christianity.

"Coming into leadership in a movement like that really young—instead of wrestling, instead of having relationships with people who thought differently—I was immediately in a context where I adopted everything. I began to advocate for everything without asking hard questions and without exploring the human experience." Shortly before telling me this, Josh had laughed about how narrow of a theological branch he and his friends had been on. "It was more like a twig," he joked.

There is something to this idea of total buy-in at an early age. It's referred to negatively as indoctrination. When we buy into a faith too early, this is an ingredient for deconversion later in life. To avoid deconversion, we need to make sure we broaden our perspectives and wrestle with our doubts and hard questions in safe environments as we grow.

Deconstructing Inside the Church and Getting Eaten Alive

The third clue that Josh gave me about the current deconstruction movement is how different it is from the previous "Emerging Church" movement that took place in the late 1990s and early 2000s. The Emerging Church movement was full of pastors and ministry leaders committed to doing church differently. Authors such as Brian McClaren and Rob Bell would be some of the poster children for the Emerging Church.[2] At the time of their rise, there was a sincerity about preserving the church as a whole. Adherents were insiders giving prophetic insights to the church. To borrow the words of Dorothy Day, "as to the Church, where else shall we go, except to the Bride of Christ, one flesh with Christ? Though she is a harlot at times, she is our Mother."[3]

The Emerging Church had a Dorothy Day about them. Today's deconstruction movement is different. This is how Josh compared the Emerging Church movement against the deconstruction people are participating in currently:

> The Emerging Church was an early wave where the same thing was happening. The difference, though, is it was happening within the church. People were saying, "We want to deconstruct this. We are still the church, but we are a better church. We are the Emerging Church." That just got attacked like it was cancer by the conservative church.
>
> It is more likely for someone who gets eaten alive inside the church to ultimately deconvert from their faith. The experience is traumatic and difficult to overcome.
>
> What is different about today's deconstruction movement is [the people deconstructing] aren't necessarily in [the church], and they don't care what you think of it.

Josh had some insights that I had never thought of. Deconstructing from the inside is entirely different from deconstructing from the outside.

My time with Josh was a gift. He and I are continuing to see where we can partner and help one another's communities move toward truth. Obviously, there are areas of disagreement, and that's okay. But his interview reinforced my findings elsewhere.

Deconstruction is likely to end in deconversion when theology is inflexible, questions aren't encouraged at an early age, and critical voices from within the church are being eaten alive. So how do we redeem the pathway of deconstruction?

In this case, we do the opposite of these three practices.

Some lessons can be learned from Joshua Harris. Others, from a dead hermit crab.

Lessons from a Dead Hermit Crab

At the mercy of my relentless eight-year-old daughter, Piper, I ended up adding another pet to the family. This time it had to be the lowest-maintenance animal, preferably with a short life span. And after skipping her weekly chores to do hours of research as to what household creature would meet this low-maintenance criterion, she landed on hermit crabs.

"You can get one too, Dad!" She exclaimed when she realized how inexpensive they were.

For months, the two hermit crabs lived in our house without demanding attention. I was pleased to find out that they were, for all intents and purposes, hermits. Self-sufficient hermits. Until one night, when our family came home to a hermit crab murder scene.

Piper walked over to the crabs, only to find the pinchers of her hermit crab lying on opposite sides of the terrarium. Her crab had been murdered! Torn into pieces by mine.

"Dad!" she yelled. "Your hermit crab killed my hermit crab."

I've been to enough counseling sessions to know that this is the type of memory that will come up when Piper is thirty years old, trying to figure out why she doesn't trust men. After a few minutes of tear-filled dialogue, we decided to go to the pet store to get her a new, still inexpensive hermit crab.

"Why did this happen?" I asked the pet-store worker.

"That's easy," they responded as they led us down the aisle to the small-pet area of the store. "Her crab outgrew its shell, and it needed a new home to go in. The only available shell it could find was your hermit crab's shell. When it tried to crawl in, your hermit crab felt threatened and cut hers into pieces."

Stopped in my tracks by the unnerving mental image of a shell-less hermit crab (don't look it up), I asked, "Well, how do we stop that from happening again?"

"Here's what you do: Place empty shells throughout the terrarium anticipating that both crabs will outgrow their homes. That way, the crabs have a safe place to grow up in once they outgrow their original shells."

Ladies and gentlemen, may I introduce you to Hermit Crab Christianity.

Hermit Crab Christianity

Is this not the daunting reality of culture? People who grew up in the church have deconstructed their worldview, outgrown the faith of their homes, and been slaughtered when trying to reenter the evangelical shell. As the body of Christ, the way forward is not refusing to let deconstructionists into the church. And, at the expense of sounding like a holy heretic, I think that if a strict apologetics approach had worked before, we wouldn't be in our present situation.

Instead, what if we practiced deconstructing—and reconstructing—our own faith? What if there is a genius behind tearing down the old before building something new? The truth is we are outgrowing our own shells. We need to deconstruct them so we can rebuild a safe Christianity that celebrates the spiritual misfit on their way in. "If you build it, they will come" may not work anymore with church buildings;[4] but it may be the way forward for interacting with the nones and dones.

We need a pathway forward that reverses the three deconversion tendencies we learned about.

We need flexible theologies.
We need to treat questions as spiritual gifts and questioning as a
spiritual discipline.

We need to allow the critics within the church to have a seat at the table. Dare I say positions on staff?

A new generation of people are searching for nonjudgmental spaces where they can question the effectiveness, usefulness, and truthfulness of Christianity. If we aren't equipped to become those spaces, we will leave the seekers of our day no other choice but to go to places that are safe for questioning.

Simply put: If the church doesn't accompany deconstructionists in their journey to reconstruct a personal relationship with Jesus, then the church will be deconstructed altogether, with no one left to rebuild with its remains.

We must become equipped to be a safe space, or the church is over. In the West, whoever can provide safety for the deconstructionist will win their trust—and, ultimately, set the trajectory for the thinking mind.

Continuing My Confession

The headlines about Josh abandoning the faith used to shake me. After talking to him, I find the headlines to be nothing more than clickbait. Almost fearmongering from the theologically conservative elitist. Instead of being fearful, we need to be curious. We need to learn the path to avoid the pitfalls. Perhaps all that "straight and narrow" talk was less about not sleeping with your boyfriend or girlfriend and more about keeping your faith in Jesus. Who would have thought!

For some, this sort of path feels like it would be too critical of the church. Too little praise, too much sorrow. And if that's your perspective of deconstruction, you're among the few who see the church as an unquestionable institution. For Christ's sake, though, we must be asking the same questions as our doubting brothers and sisters.

There is only one way to a life-giving relationship with Jesus, and it's through the valley of death. Most faiths have to die at least once so they can be resurrected. A glorified but hardly recognizable faith, I suppose. This process has taken on a variety of names over the centuries. Saint John of the Cross called it the "dark night of the soul."[5] There is an argument to be made that whole denominations have formed out of the resurrected faith of individuals and groups. For the past thirty years or so, this process has been referred to as deconstruction and reconstruction.

In an age where social media is the primary means of information and communication, there's a noticeable rallying cry around deconstructing Western evangelicalism. It's not new, per se, but it is louder than before. The self-proclaimed deconstructionists are leaving the church, leaving the faith of their childhood, and they are captivating other intellectual minds on their way out. Hopefully you're finding that it's time to participate in the world of deconstruction for yourself, unearth a fuller gospel, and reconstruct a faith that is more compelling than ever. A rare, precious faith that doubters and deconstructionists have been longing for all along.

If you are still hesitant, you are not alone. Evangelicals have equated deconstruction with destruction of faith for as long as I can remember. For most pastors and parents, deconstruction is the preliminary work of deconversion. I wish it didn't have such close associations with such words. Nevertheless, it is the path forward. Without a strategy from the church in this area, our sons and daughters are sure to veer to the right and to the left.

Is this a path you are willing to tread?

What if your faith is more Jesus centered in the end?

"A path through deconstruction?" you might say. "Why would a Christian encourage people to question their faith?"

Imagine telling a firearms instructor that they shouldn't be teaching people how to fire guns safely. *What if someone uses this class to kill another human being?* you might think to yourself, although it's a rather simplistic way of seeing the purpose of the class.

People who misuse firearms will do so with or without a class. A path through deconstruction is similar. Sure, it could end in deconversion. But the purpose of this path through deconstruction is to engage in the truth that remains when the monuments of biases and opinions are burned to ashes. Is this not the story of so many who have gone before us?

Inspiring figures of history, known and unknown soldiers, provide strong evidence that the mind of Christ is with those who are committed to reconstructing what their truth-seeking questions have torn down. Historically, Christianity is tethered to deconstructionists who are now revered as heroes. Trustworthy guides from Jesus to the apostle Paul to Martin Luther have become theological geniuses in their ability to "blow it up" and strategically rebuild with the remains.

Could it be that deconstruction is the discipline of a disciple, not an atheist?

Yes, I did say the discipline. A code of behavior practiced by Jesus' disciples. As it stands, people are unable to process the segmentation between religious tradition and coherent theology. And because there is no strategy for deconstruction, it becomes an end in itself. But deconstruction should be a means to an end; namely, the reconstruction of one's faith to be passed on with humility, stability, and a newfound personal confidence. To recap:

Without a strategy, deconstruction becomes an end.
With a strategy, it becomes a means to an end.
Reconstructing belief in a Jesus-looking God is that end.

I do hope that you feel the urgency behind these words. If you are not currently feeling the winds of culture threatening a "house of cards" theology, your loved ones and neighbors most certainly are. According to an article from *USA Today*, for every one convert to Christianity, there are four deconversions happening.[6] Although deconstruction doesn't always result in deconversion, anyone who is deconverting from Christianity has to pass through the valley of deconstruction.

Let's explore the terrain together.

Chapter 4

Deconstruction
Is about Authority

But man, proud man.
Drest in a little brief authority,
Most ignorant of what he's most assured—
His glassy essence—like an angry ape,
Plays such fantastic tricks before high heaven
As make the angels weep.

SHAKESPEARE, *MEASURE FOR MEASURE*

We're all pretty bizarre. Some of us are just better at hiding it, that's all.

ANDREW CLARK IN *THE BREAKFAST CLUB*

How would the evangelical church treat Jesus if he physically attended a Sunday morning service? I think they would treat him much like how Bruno was treated by his family in the movie *Encanto*.

Like every good Disney movie, *Encanto* calls us to be enchanted by another culture and land. This time, we are taken to Colombia. The movie is about a family that lives in a magical house that the family, the Madrigals, call the Encanto. On a certain birthday, each child receives a special power. As we meet the characters, we start to realize that the gifts the children receive vary greatly. Pepa can control the weather with her emotions, while Dolores has the gift of superhuman hearing. Camilo has the impressive ability to shape-shift, but the youngest Madrigal might have him beat. I mean, how can you one-up Antonio's ability to talk to animals (and ride a pet jaguar)! As unique as each Madrigal family member is, two of them stand out particularly: Mirabel and Bruno. Mirabel was never given a gift on her birthday. Bruno, on the other hand, has a gift that hasn't been well received. Bruno's gift feels like more of a curse to everyone who lives in the Encanto. Bruno can see the future, and his predictions are often more ominous than the family would like to accept. Ominous as they are, Bruno's predictions always come true.

Mirabel starts noticing that the Encanto is falling apart. The life source of the house is a single candle, and one night, Mirabel sees it flickering and the walls cracking. "Everything is fine!" Abuela announces at a party, but deep down the family knows something is happening.[1] Some of the children's powers are acting up, and Mirabel takes it upon herself to save the house that she loves and grew up in.

Stop for a moment.

The gifted ones want the show to keep on going, while the "ordinary" person wants to save the house. The investigative work is left up to the one who isn't preoccupied with her abilities or the crowd.

Keep that in mind.

Mirabel is convinced that the house is worth saving, but in order to save it, she needs to find Bruno. Bruno had been exiled years ago for his depressing, sometimes frightening visions, and no one knows where he went. Mirabel finds a way into the walls of the Encanto, and that's where she finds Bruno. Hiding away. Eating with the rats and acting a little crazy. But always longing for his family. We even see the inside of the kitchen wall, where he set up a table with a plate to eat with the family without them knowing. Getting as close to his family as he can without being noticed. If the other Madrigals had found out Bruno was in the walls, they would've fortified even farther to keep him out. At one point, Bruno says, "My gift wasn't helping the family, but uh . . . I love my family, you know?" In fact, he loves his family and their house. When we meet him, we find out that Bruno is patching the cracks from the inside. He doesn't want the Encanto to fall apart.

Bruno's final vision is of Mirabel and the destruction of the Encanto. "My guess," he tells her, "[is that] the family, the Encanto, the fate of the miracle itself, it's all going to come down to you."[2] Bruno's vision about the destruction of the house has a clue in it, indicating that Mirabel has to talk to her sister, Isabel. Isabel is gifted, she looks and sounds perfect, and her fantastic qualities are frustrating to Mirabel. But Mirabel ends up inviting Isabel, and all her siblings, into authenticity. True, I-have-problems authenticity. They don't have to be perfect, and they don't have to perform for the town. All of which upsets Abuela and causes the house to cave in on itself. Even though the house crumbles, Bruno's reputation is restored. He is welcomed back into the family and allowed to come out of the walls. When the house is rebuilt, it's the ordinary, nongifted, noncharismatic Mirabel whom the house welcomes in first (remember, it's a magic house).

The first time I saw this movie, it was a parable for me. I honestly, I'm surprised Jesus doesn't tell this story in any of the Gospels. I just watched it again with my kids, and I'm convinced that any message that Disney was trying to portray is dwarfed in comparison to this one main idea:

Jesus is hiding in the walls of his house.

The brothers and sisters who don't fit the family mold are finding him because they can see that the house is cracking.

And the house *is* cracking.

Cracks in the Walls

Imagine Jesus walking into a church service on a Sunday morning. Everyone starts singing to God without knowing he is there. The message is powerful, polished, and perfectly delivered with deliberate pauses after impressively wordsmithed quotes. There is enough time for a moment of reflection before the next service starts. Jesus, looking around, wonders if he should point out the cracks in the walls.

Some of the critics are right: The walls *do* have cracks in them.

None that we can see, of course. But we can all feel them. And it's in the brokenness of the current church model—not the polished parts of the building that we show to visitors—that we will find Jesus. By "we," I mean those of us who are willing to compromise comfortable seats in the house for the sake of finding Jesus in the walls.

Unless we see the world through the lens of Jesus, our view of how things are going is dangerously compromised. For thousands of years, from the walls of religious assemblies, the Jesus-looking God has been proclaiming a vision that frightens us.

> Listen to this, family of Israel,
>> this Message I'm sending in bold print, this tragic warning: . . .
>
> "I can't stand your religious meetings.
>> I'm fed up with your conferences and conventions.
> I want nothing to do with your religion projects,
>> your pretentious slogans and goals.
> I'm sick of your fund-raising schemes,
>> your public relations and image making.
> I've had all I can take of your noisy ego-music.
>> When was the last time you sang to *me*?
> Do you know what I want?
>> I want justice—oceans of it.
> I want fairness—rivers of it.
>> That's what I want. That's *all* I want."
> AMOS 5:1, 21-24, MSG

I have seen a lot of churches start in my lifetime, and I'm convinced that Jesus is allowing a radical critique of religious leaders and the way human traditions are esteemed higher than biblical truth. At no point in the New Testament is Jesus defending a model of ministry or a man of God. His life is the model, and he is the Man. All other options tend to fall on their own.

Repeating Jesus' Prediction

I'm not always sure what to make of Mark 13:1-4. It's the story of Jesus predicting the destruction of the Temple while his disciples are enamored with it. Both the prophecy and its fulfillment strike me as odd. Jesus could have stopped the Temple from being destroyed. He could have rallied the Jewish troops or told his disciples how to protect Jerusalem and the Jewish history found there. Instead, Jesus shows up as the original Bruno.

> As [Jesus] came out of the temple, one of his disciples said
> to him, "Look, Teacher, what wonderful stones and what
> wonderful buildings!" And Jesus said to him, "Do you see these
> great buildings? There will not be left here one stone upon
> another that will not be thrown down."
> And as he sat on the Mount of Olives opposite the temple,
> Peter and James and John and Andrew asked him privately, "Tell
> us, when will these things be, and what will be the sign when all
> these things are about to be accomplished?"
> MARK 13:1-4, ESV

Around thirty-seven years after Jesus' prediction, Jerusalem and the Temple were devastated. Followers of Jesus were arrested, tried, and killed at the hands of Titus Caesar. From AD 70 to 135, Roman governing officials attempted to eradicate Jewish people from the earth—and even from memory. Church historian Flavius Josephus "witnessed the siege and aftermath," documenting what he saw:

> Now as soon as the army had no more people to slay or to
> plunder, because there remained none to be the objects of their
> fury, Titus Caesar gave orders that they should now demolish
> the entire city and Temple. . . . It was so thoroughly laid even

with the ground by those that dug it up to the foundation, that
there was left nothing to make those that came thither believe
Jerusalem had ever been inhabited.[3]

Under the umbrella of Talmudic rabbis, there were two roles that
help us understand and interpret Jewish history. Those two roles were
that of the Tanna and that of the Amora. The Tannaim put together oral
traditions that were roughly (and I use that term lightly) based on the
law. The Amoraim were the expounders, the commentators of their day.
They pulled on the threads of history to unravel a meaning that would
help the Jewish people not repeat destructive behaviors of the past.[4]
The Amoraim believed that the falling of Jerusalem was God punishing
the Jewish people.[5] They had become a people who cared more about
who was right than about who was in need. In the aftermath of this
destruction, many Jews turned their back on the faith of their childhood.
Others joined the movement of Christianity. And this is where I find
Jesus' prediction disorienting.

On the one hand, you have Jesus predicting the collapse of the
Temple while his followers are fascinated by the grandiosity of it all. As
a pastor, I can never forget this lesson, never let myself get distracted
by the trappings of the world. On the other hand, the fulfillment of his
prediction caused the physical, and spiritual, death of so many. Why did
Jesus allow it? Why didn't his followers make it a priority to stop it from
happening? Why doesn't Paul pick up the slack and make it the epicenter
of his mission? Or at least begin a funding campaign to rebuild? Where
was Jesus in the destruction of the Temple? Naturally, I have so many
questions about why Jesus didn't stop the destruction of everything the
religious people of the day had built.

After reading commentaries and studying the event, I think the
destruction of the Temple was a horrific event of genocide. It was never
condoned by God, never God's idea. I do think that it was bound to
happen and that the Amoraim were onto something. God's heart, as

made known in Christ, is not an "us versus them" narrative. It's an "us for them" story! When the "us versus them" narrative is the predominant mindset of the people of God, he may allow the deconstruction of his house . . . and of the very ideas that the house was built on. The heart of God is that everyone would be brought into his house (John 14:2). When the house of God doesn't share the heart of God, it's bound to come down.

The ideologies and idols that impress us are the very things that Jesus has been deconstructing all along. And the house is still crumbling under our very eyes.

In 2021, *Christianity Today* released a podcast called *The Rise and Fall of Mars Hill*. The podcast chronicled the story of Mars Hill Church and how its pastor, Mark Driscoll, contributed to its explosive growth and exposed shortcomings. It's a podcast about how Jesus was still in the walls of the church even as it was crumbling. How staff members and volunteers found God's grace among the rubble, and how they are rebuilding companies and churches that allow the Jesus of the Bible back in. More than a history lesson, *The Rise and Fall of Mars Hill* intentionally punctured our illusions about evangelical church culture. It deconstructed the fortified castle of religious norms and challenged all of us to let Jesus be the builder of his church. Mike Cosper, host of the podcast, gives a rather instructive critique in an episode titled "Who Killed Mars Hill?" As you may recall from *Encanto*, Bruno isn't responsible for the house's demise. Here's Mike:

> If it just keeps happening, isn't there something broader to look at? Like, ourselves. When we ask why this happens, shouldn't we ask why *we* keep doing it? Why *we* seem to like charismatic figures whose character doesn't align with their gifts?[6]

In the next chapter, we'll look at what Jesus is deconstructing in evangelical Christianity. Through interviews conducted for this book, we'll find that there are three serpents in the Garden of Eden currently luring Christians away from the way God intended things to be. Here, however, I must reinforce that deconstruction is not bad. It is a practice of Jesus himself. It is a practice of his disciples. It's the practice of the Hebrew prophets. Of the martyrs and the saints throughout church history. As we will see, deconstruction is a discipline for Jesus because reconstructing the image of God in the hearts of man is his aim. Deconstruction is the way to reformation. All throughout the story of God and man, every generation needs thoughtful reformers. In her book The Great Emergence, Phyllis Tickle describes how every five hundred years the church "cleans out its attic" and holds "a giant rummage sale," inspired by the ideas of the late Anglican bishop Mark Dyer, who thought we were in one of those now.[7] The author of Hebrews put it this way:

> Don't turn a deaf ear to these gracious words. If those who ignored earthly warnings didn't get away with it, what will happen to us if we turn our backs on heavenly warnings? His voice that time shook the earth to its foundations; this time— he's told us this quite plainly—he'll also rock the heavens: "One last shaking, from top to bottom, stem to stern." The phrase "one last shaking" means a thorough housecleaning, getting rid of all the historical and religious junk so that the unshakable essentials stand clear and uncluttered.
> HEBREWS 12:25-27, MSG

The type of "shaking" that Hebrews is referring to is the type of deconstruction where Jesus and his followers use the authority of Christ to critique the world's corruption of the church and its practices. Jesus had a daring way about his deconstruction. It was always focused on who had the ultimate authority and how those in authority use their power. His parables, metaphors, teachings, and life provoked those who practiced authority or exerted power.

DECONSTRUCTION IS ABOUT AUTHORITY

Challenging Our View of Power

If Jesus is the personification of God (and I believe he is), then everything he said and did is how things are meant to be. I used to think that the Kingdom of God was an upside-down Kingdom. Turns out, it's right side up! It's the world that has capsized. This is most evident when you contrast the world's view of power with Jesus' understanding of it. In Jesus' day, people without power were mesmerized by what he did. People with power were offended by who he did it for. And unfortunately, not much has changed.

I met Stephanie in Virginia when I was putting on a Reach like Jesus Summit.[8] What is that? Think workshop meets TED Talk meets seminar. The objective of this three-hour, interactive teaching is to help church people love their non-Christian family and friends without the ulterior motive of converting them. Stephanie was one of the first people to pipe up. She was in her seventies and used her cane to help herself up when she had something to say. Stephanie thought that any other reason to befriend someone, other than converting them, would be pointless. "Eternity is on the line!" she said at one point.

"What's your name?" I asked her.

"Stephanie. My name is Stephanie, and I thought you were going to teach us evangelism."

"Tell me about the person you are hoping to evangelize." This sort of back-and-forth doesn't always prove fruitful, but it ended well. Stay with me.

"It's my daughter." Her mood visibly changed from anger to sadness. "My daughter isn't living how I want her to live, and I've tried to tell her. I've tried to tell her that she isn't pleasing God. We used to argue, and now I just keep my mouth shut." Stephanie keeping her mouth shut? I would have to see it to believe it!

I waited for a while before asking, "Were you hoping to learn a new way to evangelize your daughter?"

63

"Yes." The room was quiet. Everyone was sitting except for her. She was standing with her cane propping up her right side. Tears now rolling down both cheeks, she tried to wave me away with her left hand.

"Okay, Stephanie. What if we tried a new way of showing up for your daughter? I know you are concerned about your daughter's salvation, but that isn't up to you. Jesus lifts that burden from you by asking you only to love her well. Will you stay and we can chat at different points throughout the summit?"

She was crying too hard to answer, but she gave me a thumbs-up as she sat down.

Throughout the day, we visited on and off. I learned that she was a veteran with a real admiration for the Bible. Maybe *obsession* is a better word. Stephanie had a rather flat reading of the Bible. Everything was literal for her, and her worldview didn't have a high tolerance for mystery, paradox, or any other historically Christian postures. What Stephanie learned about power in the military had almost entirely blinded her to the meekness of Jesus. Since she viewed the Bible as the ultimate authority, she considered anyone who questioned it as rebellious or moronic. She stopped me during one of the breaks and it finally felt like we were getting somewhere.

"I used to serve in the Middle East," she shared.

"Thank you for . . ." I was interrupted again by her left hand waving at me. It seems to be how she communicates when she is emotionally vulnerable.

"One of my roles was as a prison guard for captured Muslims. We would treat them horribly. *I* would treat them horribly. Trying to make up for the way I treated them, I would throw a Bible in their cell and tell them they had to read it."

If any version of this was practiced at home, it's no wonder her daughter hates her, I thought to myself.

Stephanie continued with her confession: "The Muslims had lots of questions about the Bible, and I had no idea how to answer. 'Read it!' I would yell. I figured if we were going to kill them, the least I could do is make sure they didn't go to hell." That's when I realized that Stephanie's view of power had to be blown up. Her God was a condemning, Muslim-hating, tyrannical deity who expected her to recruit more converts or else . . . Therefore, she couldn't possibly waste time actually befriending and serving people. She was wrong, but her behavior was all making sense.

The Bible was power to her. Rank was power. Being the mom in the relationship was power. Power was to be used to tell people how to think and what to think—and (quite frankly) never to let them think on their own. In Stephanie's militaristic world, power was used to control the powerless. A sentiment shared by author Joseph Conrad. "Thinking is the great enemy of perfection," he once wrote. "The habit of profound reflection, I am compelled to say, is the most pernicious of all the habits formed by the civilized man."[9]

Stephanie and I talked at length about how Jesus used his power. I talked with her about the following verse: "Whatever you did for one of the least of these brothers and sisters of mine, you did for me" (Matthew 25:40). I told her that Jesus was referring to those in prison (25:39). It's amazing how we, Christians, can read the Bible daily and still have our hearts firmly against the ways of the Kingdom of Heaven. This is why we must always read the Bible through the lens of the crucified Christ, not the warrior God.

At the end of the Reach like Jesus Summit, Stephanie stood up again. Remember the last time this happened? Hell hath no fury like Stephanie's scorn!

She started with a different tone this time: "Preston, I only have probably ten more years of my life left. I'll be very fortunate if I have more than that. I promise to commit the remainder of my life to rec-onciling with my daughter. I have a lot of work to do, but I have to do everything I can to serve her because that's what Jesus would do!"

Sometimes I think it's more impressive when a Christian decides to follow Jesus than it is when a non-Christian confesses their sins.

Everyone stood up and started cheering for seventy-eight-year-old Stephanie. By "everyone," I mean there was probably some champagne popped in heaven. It's no small miracle when someone who used to use the Bible to shut people down now allows the Bible to shut them up. "The greatest among you shall be your servant" (Matthew 23:11, ESV). Stephanie was finally becoming someone great.

How Jesus of Them

Different versions of Stephanie's story have popped up throughout my interviews. A quick glance at history would tell us that Stephanie can serve as an archetype. The use and abuse of power is, by far, the most common reason why people are leaving the faith.[10] Should we blame people for walking away from religion when it is so intertwined with greed, oppression, manipulation, and control?

Author Philip Yancey points this out clearly: "As I read the birth stories about Jesus I cannot help but conclude that though the world may be tilted toward the rich and powerful, God is tilted toward the underdog."[11] Evangelicalism has had a long history of authoritarianism. By that, I mean a person in power wielding that power in ways that further their agenda or interpretation of Scripture. That's putting it gently. The actual definition of authoritarianism is "favoring complete obedience or subjection to authority as opposed to individual freedom."[12] Deconstruction can be found any time authoritarianism is at work. When a human interprets Scripture in a self-serving manner, it always oppresses others by making them serve that human. Unfortunately, this is present in all expressions of religion. Protestants have often criticized the Catholic church for having one pope, but evangelicals typically have a pope for every congregation—the pastor.

When we look at the things that Jesus called into question, we see they were centered around who has the authority and how that authority is being used. From the "you have heard it said, but I say unto you" passages (Matthew 5) to the woman caught in the act of adultery (John 7:53–8:11). Jesus is the only one who can properly handle power. He always uses his power to serve, not to be served. His power is given away freely just by touching his robe. His power goes unnoticed when he humbly washes his disciples' feet. His power is underestimated when he rides in on a donkey. The locals are attracted to his healing power and puzzled by his fierce resistance to exerting that power over anyone. Jesus is not intimidated by men in power but holds ground for those without power. He rebukes his disciples for wanting more power. Jesus' authority is never used to make others serve him. It is always used to make room for those who need to be served.

Now, someone could point to one particular "power" passage in the life of Christ. The incident when he flipped the tables. It's the one time I see Jesus becoming physically angry and exerting force. However, he is exerting power on behalf of those without it, and in the face of those with it. Plus, we must admit that one story about Jesus flipping tables does not justify countless stories of us denying others a place at ours. I'm certain we are sitting at tables Jesus would have flipped, and we are flipping tables he would have sat at.

This is what is so fascinating about the deconstruction movement. The entire mindset of a deconstructionist is to challenge who has the authority and how they are using it.

How Jesus of them!

Or how Bruno of them.

There is a part of the movie *Encanto* where we see Bruno sitting at a table within the walls of the house. A table that mirrors the dining room table that his family sat at for every meal, only his table was sitting among rats and dust. No one knew about the table he was sitting at every night. Yet he was still setting the table. While the family was dining without him, he was there the whole time. Longing for a seat at the table but knowing his voice wasn't welcome. It was too disrupting to their daily routines and reputation. They didn't just avoid talking about Bruno; they didn't let Bruno talk.

The Communion table has often felt this way lately. It's the one thing we're supposed to do in Jesus' remembrance. In a mysterious way, he is present with us through the bread and the wine. But unfortunately, we aren't always present with him. It's a quick part of the Sunday program. Instead, what are the things we are doing in remembrance of him?

We are voting in his name.

We are shaming in his name.

We are remembering him without letting him be present at the table, and the house is cracking.

Chapter 5

WWJD?
(What Would Jesus Deconstruct?)

A dead thing can go with the stream, but only a living thing can go against it.
G. K. CHESTERTON, *THE EVERLASTING MAN*

I don't wanna go to heaven without raising hell.
KESHA, "RAISING HELL"

THE COMBINATION OF MY EDUCATION and experience has led me to live intentionally with skeptics, doubters, and the spiritually wounded. To create room for the spiritual claustrophobia that keeps the deconstructionist out of church. Sometimes that takes me to a coffee shop or bar to lead a Doubters' Club meeting. Other times, I'll find myself on a university campus. I have found myself in some incredibly hostile environments when it comes to defending the faith, but there is always one subject that unites the room. Conservative and progressive minds seem to feel curious about the person of Jesus, and I'll take curiosity over conspiratorial or conniving ideas all day.

This was certainly the case when I visited the University of North Carolina. I had flown in for a short time to help train a Chi Alpha group on how to start a Doubters' Club. They asked me to speak at one of their campus ministry gatherings while I was there. "Speak on whatever you want," they told me. "Can you end it with a Q and A?"

"What type of Q and A are you wanting?" I asked.

"You know . . . the kind where students can ask anything and you give them the answer."

This made me laugh. I don't think people know that I have more questions than the average critic when it comes to Christianity. I live and breathe this thing. My prayers end with more question marks than periods. My questions are like the credits at the end of a movie—never-ending, from all over the place, and hard to articulate.

"Okay. You do know that I don't have all the answers, right?" I was quick to set up some realistic expectations.

Fast-forward to the event. The message was over, we closed in prayer, and then I talked briefly about how questions are the royal road to enlightenment. Who doesn't want to feel more enlightened than they did when they arrived?

"Let's wrestle with God together," I told the room. "Who has a question?"

If we are ever on the University of North Carolina campus together, I can take you to the exact seat where Bryce was sitting. From where I was standing, he was in the back right, last row, three seats from the left end.

"Hey, Preston. My name is Bryce,[1] and I'm an atheist. I saw a flier for tonight's event. It's my first time."

"Thanks for joining us, Bryce. I'm sure you have a lot of questions. What feels most pressing for you? What question would you like to throw out there?" As I was saying this, Bryce stood up. Straightening his backward hat and pulling out his notepad, he was ready to talk.

"I have a lot of questions," he said. "Let's start with this one: How can you think religion is helpful, at all, when so much bad has been done in the name of God?"

Bryce listed a few of the blemishes of our past. Honestly, I think it's worse than he thinks it is. So that's what I told him.

"Thanks for bringing it up, but I think the problem is worse than you think."

The crowd looked at me as if I were crazy. Like I mentioned earlier, I have more questions than most people in the room. Which might be why my relationships with skeptics tend to be so steady.

I listed a few of the deformities that have grown on the body of Christ. From genocide in the Old Testament to the Crusades to white supremacy. "All done with a word from God," I told him.

"Exactly!" Bryce exclaimed. Quickly followed by: "Wait. Why are you a Christian, then?"

I smiled. That question is my favorite setup to talk about the centrality of Jesus, but we weren't there yet. We had one more layer to peel back first.

"Before I answer that question, Bryce, let me ask you something. Why didn't you make this question personal? Why are you talking about the injustices done in the past? Surely you have experiences about how Jesus followers have treated you."

"That's true," he said. "I can't reconcile the alignment evangelicals have with right-wing politics. I've been told I'm going to hell because I'm gay. Damn. There is more hate coming from the church than from hell itself."

Reread that last sentence.

One more time.

Now, it's time to talk about Jesus.

In front of the entire room, Bryce and I talked about Jesus. The love of God portrayed through the person of Jesus. The way Jesus deconstructed false views of God and offered hope to the world. Before moving to the next student with questions, I told Bryce, "I think the church is looking at itself in the mirror and we are realizing we don't look like the One we claim to follow. I hope you consider following Jesus based on his life, not the lives of his followers." If Bryce decides to follow Jesus, it will be straight into deconstruction. A place Jesus is very comfortable in.

No matter what worldview a person decides to adopt, they will always have to say something about the person of Christ. This intrigues me. How enamored we all are by this man. The nature of his life wasn't spectacular. Jesus was not the most impressive character in history, but he was the most impactful. An unavoidable character that the thinking individual must do something with. Volumes have been written on Jesus, and volumes are still to be published. The disciple John wasn't kidding when he wrote, "Jesus did many other things as well. If every one of them were written down, I suppose that even the whole world would not have room for the books that would be written" (John 21:25). We clearly will never stop having things to say about the life and ministry of Jesus! Even acclaimed atheist and author Bart Ehrman says that he doesn't know of a scholar of antiquity who doesn't believe that Jesus was a historical figure worth examining.[2]

Jesus doesn't just stand out in history; he stands out in the present. To follow Jesus in the twenty-first century is to follow him out of certain evangelical norms. To deconstruct these temples of idolatry, and to call others to do the same.

Issues Worthy of Deconstructing

In the interviews and research I conducted for this book, many different evangelical norms came up as issues that Christians are deconstructing today. Some of the big ones were politics, purity culture, a "flat" reading of the Bible, the treatment and exclusion of the LGBTQ+ community, the doctrine of hell, and hypocrisy. All of these issues were attached to personal stories. People's objections to Christianity are never purely intellectual. Their doubts and disbeliefs are seeds planted in the soil of the heart, where stories are remembered.

I'm not going to touch on every issue in this book, and I'm intentionally not making a statement on many of the issues that many deconstructionists are deconstructing. For one, this is a book about the value of deconstructing faith, not about what exactly you should believe. Secondly, I don't want to lose any readers or reinforce your preferred reading of Scripture. In either case, I am not holding ground for the skeptic in your life. I've come to accept that to the conservative I'm too liberal, and to the liberal I'm too conservative.

However, I do want to address two areas where I think Jesus is blowing up the mountain, as they have come to light in recent years as major stumbling blocks for Christians. These two issues are politics and purity culture. I will use them as examples of how our Christian culture can sometimes miss the point of Christianity and why people are asking questions about a better way forward.

Politics and a Trump Kind of Christian

There are three major positions when it comes to how Christians have historically engaged with politics.[3] First, some Christians believe that it is their job to inform, and change, culture by engaging with (or gaining) political power. In this view, Christians see it as their duty to practice the authority of Christ on earth through the rules and laws that are put in place. "On earth as it is in heaven" is accomplished by enforcing righteous laws that reflect God and Scripture (Matthew 6:10). Lobbying for candidates and causes is based on who will implement God's law through human laws.

Second, some Christians view their role in politics through a two-kingdom lens. They see the separation of church and state as a clear line that God has established, with two separate aims for each kingdom. According to this view, "the purpose of secular government is to keep sin in check and rule over sinners by force. The purpose of the church is to transform sinners into saints who do not need to be ruled by law."[4] This view gives the most allowance for ecumenical thought when it comes to whether a Christian should, or should not, become political. Believe it or not, there used to be a time when Christians were allowed to think differently on political engagement.

The third group of people is of the opinion that Christians should distance themselves as far as possible from political involvement. This group would be in opposition to the first, and their convictions are based in a "citizen of heaven" mindset. Their view is explained by a ReKnew article as follows:

> Christians are called to be loyal to Christ's kingdom alone and to see themselves as citizens and ambassadors of the kingdom of God while living in a "foreign" land (Phil 3:20). The present world, including its political systems, is under the control of Satan. Therefore, trying to conform it to God's will is futile and even dangerous. The power of the gospel is found in offering an alternative way of living, not in influencing the political process.[5]

Both times Donald Trump ran for president (especially the second time), we saw a fourth group form, one that is more militaristic than the first and more fundamental than either end of the political spectrum. This fourth group has existed since the 1950s but always under the guise of one of the other three groups. Ironically, Trump became the pride flag of this group's coming-out party. This group is often referred to as the evangelical right.

The evangelical right has traded spouses. They have traded being the bride of Christ for the bride of Trump. And the evangelical right has defended the abusive tendencies of her spouse with sentiments that suggest "everything done is a means to an end." Trump's character, brashness, sexism, racism, and clear "us versus them" worldview is only a means to an end. What's the end?

Me and my country.

In that order.

Which is the exact opposite of the Christian worldview.

Christians see others first, and we are living for another country.

Truly, his heart beats for the American people, the evangelical right has told itself. But it's thought this without noticing that prioritizing the good of the American people, by all means necessary, is a violent assault on the Kingdom of Heaven, where all nations, tribes, and tongues will worship God (Revelation 7:9). "American people" is even a delusional phrase. America is a diverse, and divided, nation. Which American person was Trump prioritizing? It certainly wasn't the one in poverty or the one looking to make America their new home. Trump's first campaign was built on the promise of lower taxes for the rich and higher walls for the immigrant. Don't you remember his first campaign? "Make America Great Again," he touted.

America has a shockingly intemperate past. When Trump said "again," which past was he referring to? The genocidal establishment of our country or the intolerant, racist segregationists' past? Even to land somewhere in-between is disappointing on all counts. The evangelical right didn't interpret these words the same way that I do as I'm writing them. They interpreted Trump's campaign, and all his arrogant vernacular, as protecting their rights and their country. You read that right.

Christians who vote based on their rights and their country.

The evangelical right was a large voting base for Trump, and he knew it. Trump knew that he had to appeal to this group of people to tip the scales in his favor. In fact, it was Jerry Falwell Jr., the former president of Liberty University, who largely contributed to Trump's success with this fourth group. Politico reports that in the past, Falwell refused to publicly support any political candidate over fear of Liberty University losing its nonprofit status.[6] His endorsement could easily be tied to the university's, and that would put the organization in a compromising position. Apparently, these concerns faded in Falwell's mind in 2016, when he publicly endorsed Donald Trump.[7] Falwell called Trump "a successful executive and entrepreneur, a wonderful father and a man who I believe can lead our country to greatness again."[8] An endorsement like this served as a green light for other prominent evangelical leaders to follow suit. And in a hierarchical setup where the pastor serves as the man of God, what the pastor says is often seen as a word from God. So when Falwell "pumped millions of the nonprofit religious institution's funds into Republican causes and efforts to promote the Trump administration,"[9] he blurred the lines just enough for members of the evangelical right to feel like it was their Christian duty to vote for Trump.

If you've paid attention to Liberty University and the scandals surrounding the Falwells, you'll remember that Jerry resigned in August of 2021. The accusations of cover-ups, hypocrisy, misuse of funds, and sexual misconduct were coming to light, but the damage had already been done. Evangelicals knew about Trump's character, but they didn't care. "We aren't electing a pastor," they'd say. "We're electing a president."

Sam, a recovering Christian, talked with me about the Trump era. "They thought they were electing a president," he told me. "In all actuality, they were electing a savior. One who would use the Bible to continue oppressing those who weren't like them."

Sam's feelings are shared by many former evangelicals. Today, they call themselves exvangelicals. In fact, the term *exvangelical* originated from a deconstructionist who recognized how politics were corrupting Christianity in the West. Religious studies professor Bradley Onishi explains:

> Blake Chastain started the #exvangelical hashtag in 2016. Chastain grew up in a strict conservative evangelical community and felt a call to ministry during high school. During his first year of college at Indiana Wesleyan University in 2001, his religious and political views began to change. Some of his doubt formed in reaction to the invasion of Iraq and the way evangelicals supported George W. Bush's hawkish policies. After a prolonged period of questioning, Chastain left evangelicalism. He now attends an Episcopal church, though he identifies as an "agnostic to some degree."[10]

In October, AD 312, Emperor Constantine was praying as he prepared to lead his army into the Battle of Milvian. When he looked upward, he saw a cross with an inscription that said, "CONQUER BY THIS."[11] Ever since then, Christianity has had an inevitable entanglement with politics. We have reversed the commands of Christ. No longer do we give to God what is God's and to Caesar what is Caesar's (Matthew 22:21). Instead, we give to God what is Caesar's and Caesar what is only God's. We pay God what he is due in order to have a right to stand with him, meanwhile giving our ultimate allegiance to the president.

Not only would Jesus deconstruct the ideologies and practices behind the evangelical right, but man ruling over one another was never something that God wanted to construct in the first place. In the case of any political party, leveraging the words of Jesus for political power and validation is wicked and confusing. In 1 Samuel, we are told how government got started, and it was never God's ideal situation.

The Israelites were pleading with Samuel for a king. Samuel was growing old, and they were afraid that his authority and influence would be passed down to his sons, Joel and Abijah. The only problem was that his sons were after "dishonest gain and [they] accepted bribes and perverted justice" (1 Samuel 8:3). Do you see the irony in the origin of God's people craving a political leader and where we find ourselves today?

> When they said, "Give us a king to lead us," this displeased
> Samuel; so he prayed to the LORD. And the LORD told him:
> "Listen to all that the people are saying to you; it is not you
> they have rejected, but they have rejected me as their king. As
> they have done from the day I brought them up out of Egypt
> until this day, forsaking me and serving other gods, so they
> are doing to you. Now listen to them; but warn them solemnly
> and let them know what the king who will reign over them will
> claim as his rights.
> 1 SAMUEL 8:6-9

"We see that people want human rulers only because *they no longer trust God to rule*," Greg Boyd explains, which "suggests that the very existence of governments is evidence of human rebellion."[12] In the second part of the book, we will look at how to best move forward when there are clearly parts of Christianity (namely evangelicalism) that need to be deconstructed. For now, it's important to develop the deepest conviction that people will never be able to rule over others without falling prey to corruption, manipulation, and personal gain. Yes, it's true that Paul tells us in the book of Romans that all authority is put in place by God and for the purpose of order (13:1). Never are we told to trust that authority, however, or to tell others to trust them alongside us. At the end of the day, *all human authoritative governing structures are antithetical to the Christlike posture that will, in fact, change the world.*

> Jesus called them together and said, "You know that the rulers of the Gentiles lord it over them, and their high officials exercise authority over them. Not so with you. Instead, whoever wants to become great among you must be your servant, and whoever wants to be first must be your slave—just as the Son of Man did not come to be served, but to serve, and to give his life as a ransom for many."
> MATTHEW 20:25-28

As a native New Mexican, I remember when evangelicals were fighting to keep the Ten Commandments outside of the Bloomfield courthouse.[13] We shouldn't have been fighting for the Ten Commandments. We should have been fighting for the Sermon on the Mount. That's what Jesus would have done.

Purity Culture

"If you want a guy to speak to your heart, don't show him your parts."

I heard the above statement numerous times in youth group and at youth camps. Worse, I've said that statement to a crowd of young men and women a few times. Never will I ever say those words again, and I'll do everything I can to raise my two daughters in a church that recognizes the damage of purity culture. Of all the women I've talked to who are deconstructing—or reconstructing—their Christianity, purity culture came up 100 percent of the time.

Meet Anna.

Anna grew up in an evangelical household. Daughter of a pastor, Anna always tried to be on her best behavior. She has since moved away from the rural town she grew up in. Visiting her family requires a lot of work with a counselor and reemphasizing boundaries. Anna isn't very keen on church culture anymore, but she is still interested in Jesus. She cuts hair for a living and uses conversations with her clients as therapy.

"It's healing to me, you know?" she told me. "I like talking with people about their experiences and how they grew up. Here in the Midwest it almost always goes back to religion. Religion is the source of so much hurt. Most of my clients have a religious background."

Anna was trying to eat her burrito from the coffee shop next door. Doing an interview while on your lunch break isn't easy. "I know your background is religious as well, Anna. Tell me where you are spiritually now and what got you there."

She swallowed her bite, then responded, "As you know, I'm the daughter of a preacher. My family knew I was different, but they always tried to put me into certain categories that were safe for their reputation. Even allowing me to call myself a 'tomboy' in public was a stretch for them."

"So what was the straw that finally broke the camel's back for you?" I asked.

"Are you familiar with purity culture?" she asked. I merely raised my eyebrows to indicate I was listening. "It began in the nineties when churches started emphasizing the need for abstinence at all cost. We [evangelical youth] got purity rings, went to purity conferences, and were told to repent of our bad thoughts on a weekly basis. It was always part of the altar call. I always had to dress a certain way. I could never wear anything that would make a boy stumble. As if it was *my* fault they couldn't control themselves. Of all the teachings on purity that I heard, the messaging was always the same: 'My body will make others sin if I don't conduct myself properly' and 'I'm impure for having desires that are natural.' Then when my parents found out I was pregnant . . . things were never the same."

"Anna, your ten o'clock is here," the receptionist said.

"Sorry, Preston, but is there anything else?" she asked.

I had one more question before the end of her break. I have heard horror stories with the purity movement as the culprit before, and I have always wondered one thing.

"One more question. Are you finding Jesus' message about purity to be different from what you heard growing up?"

Her eyes glanced at the clock as she stood up to head over to the check-in desk. A giant smile came across her face before she responded.

"Yeah. Jesus doesn't benefit from my purity, and he isn't talking about it all the time. Come to think of it, maybe the reason all of us youth couldn't wait until marriage is because it was talked about every week."

Anna's right. Purity culture is obsessed with oversexualizing thoughts and intentions. And it's a slippery slope. Most evangelicals I talked to recognize the dangers of the messaging, but they quickly counter any concern by pointing to the only other alternative they can think of.

What about STDs?

Or unwanted pregnancies?

In *Pure: Inside the Evangelical Movement That Shamed a Generation of Young Women and How I Broke Free*, Linda Klein speaks of purity culture as a shame-based, obsessive subculture that is not, in fact, talking about the healthy boundaries of sex and marriage.

Purity culture also teaches that women are responsible for the sexual thoughts, feelings and choices men make, and so must dress, walk and talk in just the right way so as not to "inspire" sexual thoughts, feelings, and actions in them.[14]

I remember hearing sermons about sexual purity when I was growing up. In one object lesson, our sexuality was likened to chewing gum. "Everyone wants the gum before it's chewed," the youth pastor would say. "Look at the wrapper it's in. Doesn't it look so good!"

Then, he threw the gum in his mouth and gave a twenty-minute sermon about God's intent for sexuality. He concluded the message by pulling the chewed gum out. "Now who wants this?" he asked. "All chewed up. No one wants it after it has been used." The altars were filled that night. No one wanted to be seen as chewed up and worthless. Yet all of us were.

Deconstructionists have been debriefing the effects of purity culture in the shadows of the church for a while now. While the church is worried about people deconstructing, the deconstructionists are sharing stories about the destruction the church has caused. You can hardly scroll through the Instagram page of a former Christian without hearing about the effects of purity culture. Advocates of a new way forward have taken to social media to share the heartbreaking stories of those who now have Religious Trauma Syndrome. This is a condition "experienced by people who are struggling with leaving an authoritarian, dogmatic religion and coping with the damage of indoctrination."[15] It doesn't matter how the message was *meant* to be portrayed. What matters is that an entire generation heard it—and they're still suffering the effects. Girls and boys heard two damaging messages. The messaging was more pronounced for girls than it was for boys, probably because men were the ones controlling the message.

Here is what many girls heard: You are responsible for keeping the men in the church from stumbling. Modesty is a doctrine equal to the divinity of Christ. Actually, it's maybe more important. We would rather you question Jesus than show your midriff on a Wednesday night. Promiscuity is a sin that makes you undesirable. Sexual sin will make it impossible for you to have a meaningful, intimate relationship with anyone in the future. If someone wronged you sexually, what you were wearing and how you were acting contributed to their decision to do so.

Purity culture wasn't just trying to defend abstinence and a conservative sexual ethic; it was a business built on shame and regret. This became obvious to me when I realized that the messaging stopped short of the marriage bed. Purity culture had a lot to say when it came to what not to do but not much to say that pertained to the exciting sexual intimacy that married couples should be experiencing. This is why I know—beyond a shadow of a doubt—that Jesus would deconstruct purity culture.

> "Teacher," they said to Jesus, "this woman was caught in the act of adultery. The law of Moses says to stone her. What do you say?"
>
> ... [Jesus said,] "All right, but let the one who has never sinned throw the first stone!" Then he stooped down again and wrote in the dust.
>
> When the accusers heard this, they slipped away one by one, beginning with the oldest, until only Jesus was left in the middle of the crowd with the woman. Then Jesus stood up again and said to the woman, "Where are your accusers? Didn't even one of them condemn you?"
>
> "No, Lord," she said.
>
> And Jesus said, "Neither do I. Go and sin no more."
>
> JOHN 8:4-5, 7-11, NLT

When the woman was caught in the act of adultery, she wasn't given an object lesson. When Jesus met the Samaritan woman at the well, he didn't tell her that she was losing her ability to have true intimacy with her future husband. Even the lineage of Christ uniquely makes the "impure" harlot a hero. I am convinced that Jesus will always deconstruct any system built around exercising religious power over another. Additionally, he will push up against any messaging or method that is built on perpetuating shame.

Imagine Jesus walking around holding a sign that says Shame Free. The crowd of people he is walking with also have signs but theirs say Free Shame. If we aren't careful, we'll think the signs look similar, but they contain opposing messages. That's purity culture in a nutshell.

How Did Jesus Blow It Up?

Politics and purity culture are just two examples of what Jesus would blow up to establish his face in the side of the mountain. As I mentioned earlier, there are many more topics like these that we need to reconsider. You might be hearing some of the issues come up in your church or even in your family.

One of the things I realized in writing this book is how compromised people may feel as they reconsider their views on topics such as LGBTQ+, how they read the Bible, and the doctrine of hell. To change our views on any of these issues means we're giving up truth in the name of grace, or so it can feel. If that's you, please consider the following as you navigate the rest of this book: *If Jesus didn't emphasize it, we shouldn't hold it tightly.*

What did the thief on the cross think about the controversial issues of his day? What was his theology on the doctrine of hell or the inspiration of Scripture? Who knows. All I know is that there were two men on crosses that day; only one of them was receptive to Jesus.

> One of the criminals who hung there hurled insults at him: "Aren't you the Messiah? Save yourself and us!"
>
> But the other criminal rebuked him. "Don't you fear God," he said, "since you are under the same sentence? We are punished justly, for we are getting what our deeds deserve. But this man has done nothing wrong."
>
> Then he said, "Jesus, remember me when you come into your kingdom."

Jesus answered him, "Truly I tell you, today you will be with me in paradise."

LUKE 23:39-43

Did you notice how Luke wrote about the first man hanging on the cross? He wanted Jesus to save himself. "Are you not the powerful one?" he said to Jesus. "If so, save yourself and save us. Make the trial of this moment go away by proving your power" (author's paraphrase). I believe the mentality of this man toward Jesus was "Prove yourself." It's the same mentality we have when we don't like the torture of the moment. The same feeling we get when certain doctrines are called into question. The interrogation that feels like a crucifixion. We tend to see how we can prove ourselves to the one who is questioning us. But this first character? He isn't the one portrayed favorably.

The second thief on the cross has a different disposition toward Jesus. We don't know this man's thoughts or views on the debatable issues of the day, but we know he wants to live on in Jesus' heart. "Remember me when you come into your kingdom," he requests. It's as if his longing for Jesus is more important than correct theology about Jesus' person, power, or mission. When you compare the two thieves on the cross, one has right theology while the other has desperation. Which one of these criminals does Jesus invite to be with him forever?

There are stories to be unearthed before the truth can take root. Perhaps this is why apologetics isn't convincing as many people as we anticipated. How do we unearth the heart?

Together.

Christians and non-Christians.

With the same strategy that Jesus used.

Spiritual dynamite in hand.

That's what the rest of this book is about: How did Jesus deconstruct? Continuing with the analogy of Mount Rushmore, the following chapters will walk you through the acronym FUSE. The goal is that you would have the steps you need to blow up the mountain of religion until it looks like the face of Jesus.

The next time someone in your life says, "I'm deconstructing the faith," here's what you tell them:

"Let's light the FUSE!"

PART TWO

How to Deconstruct

The FUSE Method

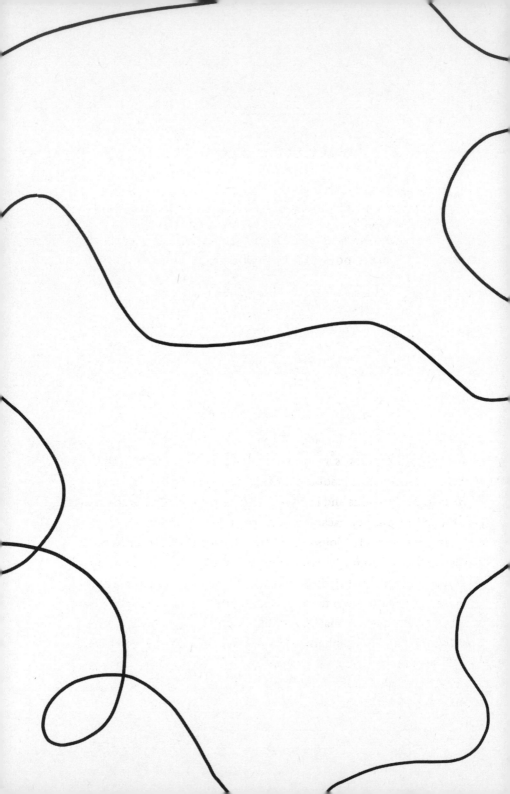

Chapter 6

F: Find the Specifics

There are those whose spiritual walk has carried them to a whole other country, where sanctity is not about minding one's morals but about being filled with "goodness." . . . These people do not even dwell on "goodness" as such; they are "too busy looking at the source from which it comes."

DAVID DOWNING, *INTO THE REGION OF AWE*

You could spend your whole life waiting for the mountain to move, but it's waiting on you.

JONNY LANG, "MAKE IT MOVE"

THIS ILLUSTRATION HAS TO DO WITH ALCOHOL. Now would be a good time to suspend your tradition for the sake of seeing Jesus more clearly. He talked about wine and made it a main element of Communion. But if they'd had whiskey back in his day . . .

In May of 2021, I joined three friends on a road trip to Kentucky. Darren flew in from Montana, and the rest of us met at Andy's house to ride together. At the time, we all had a trivial interest in bourbon whiskey. By that I mean that we liked the taste and had collected a few bottles. Just enough to make the neighbors think we knew what we were doing. Each of our neighborhoods would hold bottle shares and tastings, and we wanted to grow our knowledge and passion for the craft. Like true rookies, we climbed into Andy's new Telluride, FaceTimed our kids, and set the GPS for Louisville.

Kentucky is home to 95 percent of the world's bourbon. The original distilleries started there, and the climate is very accommodating when it comes to aging corn, wheat, barley, and rye in a barrel. There are distinct seasons for the wood to expand and contract, which enhances the flavor and greatly affects the product. The whiskey goes in the barrel clear, but it gets its golden amber color from the length of time it stays barreled.[1] Our goal on this trip was to taste some of the deepest shades of amber while contemplating God's outrageous plans for our lives. Learn, taste, and listen.

Absorbing experiences like this with close friends makes a trip more enchanting. We visited multiple distilleries, had private tours, and learned more than we had anticipated. Like this random fact: Rumor has it that a Baptist preacher by the name of Elijah Craig was the first to create bourbon. He wanted to preserve his excess corn, but he had to mash it and barrel it to send it across the sea. Who would have thought?

On our final night in Kentucky, we walked into a local liquor store where we were surprised to learn that the cashier was a whiskey sommelier. She was a trained and knowledgeable whiskey expert. She taught us that no whiskey lover should use the term "smooth" when describing the taste. The age of the whiskey deserves more respect than that. When tasting bourbon, wine, coffee, or any other craft drink, broad terms are not helpful. Instead, get specific! To help us understand, she showed us a bourbon tasting wheel, which helps you identify the specific note you are tasting.

Starting with broad categories, the wheel offers more tasting notes than you would naturally be able to come up with. For example, imagine detecting hints of fruit. The wheel would narrow it down to citrus, fresh fruit, dried fruit, or cooked fruit. From there it would get even more precise. Are you enjoying oranges, marmalade, apricot, or mince pies? (I have yet to have a bourbon that reminded me of mince pie, and I don't think I'm missing out.) I'm certain that Elijah Craig didn't come up with the bourbon wheel, but the principle behind it feels much like a Christian discipline.

The longer bourbon has aged, the more complexity it has. And the more complexity it has, the longer it may take to deconstruct the taste. A similar notion applies to the process of deconstructing a complex faith. We may know that something feels wrong, but oftentimes it's hard to pinpoint exactly what it is. The experiences I learned from Kentucky were so helpful that I translated the idea into a tool for the deconstructing mind.

I created what I call the Deconstructing Wheel. It's meant to help you, or someone you love, as they break down the specific problem they have with the faith.

This principle of "complexity over time" came up in my interviews. Just as bourbon gets more complex the longer it ages in the barrel (a four-year-old whiskey tastes much different from a fifteen-year-old one), the longer the ideas were "barreled" in someone's head, the more complex the ideas became. My hope is that the Deconstruction Wheel helps you not feel intimidated. But it will take more time and patience the longer it's been mulled over. For example, talking to a four-year-old about hell is very different from talking to a forty-year-old. The four-year-old may have a problem worrying that their friend who died went to hell, but the forty-year old has a problem with a God who would send them there.

The specifics are the starting point. There is more to be done if we are going to have a fully formed strategy. Once the specifics are verbalized, we have to understand where the idea came from.

Is the idea being deconstructed biblical?

Is it cultural?

Or is it something we believe because it benefits us?

All these questions, and more, are necessary in the journey.

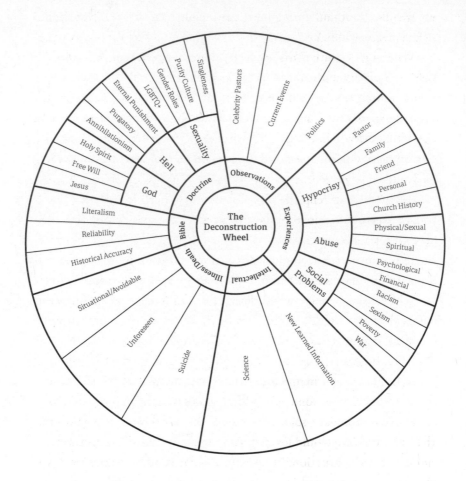

The above wheel is meant to help you as you start the deconstruction journey with a doubter or skeptic. It doesn't give you any of the answers to even the most basic apologetic questions. In fact, this Deconstruction Wheel can sometimes feel like a theological splinter to the evangelical mind. It annoyingly names what we often avoid and demands that it be dealt with. If you find yourself feeling this way, remember that the desire behind all deconstruction is discovery. Isn't that the true desire behind every Christian mind as well? As I have used the Deconstruction Wheel with my friends, I've found it's helpful to make yourself familiar with the wheel before meeting with the doubter or skeptic as you embark on this together.

When I meet with someone who is considering leaving Christianity behind, I often tell them a version of the following:

"I don't ever want you to feel like your views of Christianity and faith don't matter. I am sure you have good reasons as to why you think the way you do. Would you be willing to deconstruct evangelical Christianity with me so that we both can better understand each other? In fact, I want you to lead this. What is it about Christianity that turned you off any sort of religion?"

At this point, it's up to you to guide them into a personal story or specific objection. Be careful not to corner someone into your way of thinking, and don't retaliate frustration with other angry emotions. Absorb the pain and confusion with them and for them. Don't make it worse.

To do this well, you must know the specifics that are under interrogation. What areas of Christianity are being deconstructed?

What is causing them to laugh?

What is causing them to cry?

What is causing them to become suspicious?

When talking to someone who is questioning the faith, don't settle for blanket statements such as "I'm just deconstructing Christianity." If that were true, we would lose everyone to the feeble whims of the mere notion of deconstruction. No one can deconstruct an entire tradition that is so deeply rooted in history and culture. The human soul alone has too many possible interactions with God to give up on faith entirely. As David Benner said in *The Gift of Being Yourself*:

> Body and soul contain thousands of possibilities out of which
> you can build many identities. But in only one of these will
> you find your true self that has been hidden in Christ for all
> eternity. Only in one will you find your unique vocation and
> deepest fulfillment.[2]

For those who are deconstructing, we must give continuous attention to the parts, not the whole. That is where the difference lies between deconstruction and destruction. Destruction is to blow the whole thing up without regard for what may be true or helpful. Deconstruction, on the other hand, is to blow it up in parts. With full anticipation that, although it all feels like a tragedy, there is more at work. Even the famed atheist Sam Harris knows better than to have deconstructed Christianity. When asked by an interviewer what he has against religion, Harris responded:

> It's not so much religion, per se, it's false certainty that worries me, and religion just has more than its fair share of false certainty or dogmatism. I'm really concerned when I see people pretending to know things they clearly cannot know.[3]

I'm concerned with the same thing. One of the signs that you have encountered God is that you walk with a limp, not a strut. Religious folk pretend to know way too much, but so do the nonreligious. Deconstructing Christianity is a claim of certainty far beyond anyone's capabilities. Deconstructing part of Christianity is the actual play we find ourselves in. Finding the specifics keeps us tethered to the whole, and that is why it is the first step in deconstruction.

Jesus as the Model Deconstructionist

I want to make it clear that I am not joining the great cloud of pessimists who treat Christianity with contempt or disdain. Nor am I willing to hedge my bets on the way we currently practice Christianity in the West. Something has to give. We find ourselves in a time when tradition and God are synonymous in many people's eyes. Even Jesus had to find the specifics if he was to help people see a clearer picture of God.

Jesus deconstructed specific areas of Jewish norms to help people see God more clearly. He wasn't after abolishing the Law or the Prophets; however, the old wine had run out (Matthew 5:17; 9:14-17). The way to God was through him, and there was no room for religious assumptions or human tradition. The book of Mark shares a story about Jesus getting specific in his deconstruction of the Jewish practices of his day. Specifically, in the area of human tradition. Humanity's tradition had become entangled with God's commandments, and the picture of a Jesus-looking God had been skewed. It's a great example of when Jesus uses this principle of finding the specifics to help parse out what is useful and truthful for those outside religion. Mark's record of this account starts with Pharisees and other religious authorities gathering around to critique the way of Jesus' disciples. A spiritual gift still practiced today. And this is when you know that the Deconstructing Savior is about to put his cape on . . .

Every time the authority of human tradition is a hindrance to people living free and abundant lives, the authority of Jesus is about to deconstruct.

> The Pharisees and some of the teachers of the law who had come from Jerusalem gathered around Jesus and saw some of his disciples eating food with hands that were defiled, that is, unwashed. (The Pharisees and all the Jews do not eat unless they give their hands a ceremonial washing, holding to the tradition of the elders. When they come from the marketplace they do not eat unless they wash. And they observe many other traditions, such as the washing of cups, pitchers and kettles.)
> MARK 7:1-4

The tradition of their elders. That is a fascinating way to put it. Aren't our elders supposed to set the trajectory for how we practice our faith? They pass on the fundamentals of their denomination. They set up beliefs and behaviors for church staff and membership. They offer interpretations for our most important texts. They, the elders, certainly have a place in Christianity. Yet, they, the elders, are not the arbiters of truth.

All that said, I do wish my kids would wash their hands more. Maybe they should memorize Mark 7:2. And maybe I should memorize Mark 7:8: "You have let go of the commands of God and are holding on to human traditions."

> The Pharisees and teachers of the law asked Jesus, "Why don't your disciples live according to the tradition of the elders instead of eating their food with defiled hands?" He replied, "Isaiah was right when he prophesied about you hypocrites; as it is written:

>> 'These people honor me with their lips,
>>   but their hearts are far from me.
>> They worship me in vain;
>>   their teachings are merely human rules.'

> You have let go of the commands of God and are holding on to human traditions."
> MARK 7:5-8

Notice what Jesus does in his encounter with the Pharisees and scribes. He doesn't attack any other part of their theology. Nor does he dismantle them as hypocritical leaders (although other accounts would suggest that they were). Jesus doesn't even debate the rabbinic norms of the day. Jesus *names the specific idea that is not helpful.* In the chapters that follow, I will exegete this same passage. It will be the anchor text for us to look at how Jesus thoughtfully blows up the mountain. For now, we will stop at verse 8. Letting go of the commands of God and holding on to the traditions of man is the chief sin under investigation in the exvangelical world.

In his book *After Evangelicalism*, Dr. David Gushee thoroughly examines the traditional way we've done things in order to recommend a new path forward. A type of reconstruction outside the traditions, and traditional mindsets, of evangelical Christianity.

An appeal to the ancient Tradition to guard evangelical boundaries and set definitions certainly has been a feature of recent decades. Conservative evangelical leaders find it helpful to cite "what the church has always and everywhere believed" in their battles against dissenters. It is indeed powerful ammunition when one can cite not *sola scriptura*, but Scripture and Tradition, to support one's positions.[4]

Think about it. Many of the hills that we have died on are so far from the hill of the cross that the leap from our preferences and tradition to Golgotha is impossible for the intellectual. Only our blood is shed on the hill of our tradition. Jesus had no interest in dying for legalistic ways of living.

I was reminded of this during an interview I had with Justin Brierly, host of the podcast *Unbelievable?*, and one of his guests, Gaia. Gaia is an atheist who made it clear that her deconversion journey began when she started to notice all the rules that came with being a Christian.

"When I was in the Catholic church, one of the things that I got caught up on was the rules," she told Justin and me. Later, she talked about her experience in Protestant churches.

"I was also really appalled that this [the rules] was a mechanism to control people. There were also so many other rules that controlled. I just felt like, *I just can't do this anymore*. And I went to Protestant churches and I found that there were *other* unique rules and hoops to jump through."[5]

We can hardly expect every Christian to submit to God's commands over their legalistic tradition. But when we find specific ideas that need to be deconstructed, we must be willing to do so. I've preached the Mark 7 text in just about every size congregation imaginable. It is always met with "amens" and compliments of the sort. But in reality, not much happens. We are still victims of the oral law like those who adhered to the Talmud. The Mishnah, a collection of Jewish traditions in the Talmud, records, "It is a greater offense to teach anything contrary to the voice of the Rabbis than to contradict Scripture itself."[6] It still feels that way.

Pastors still judge those who drink alcohol.

Parents still think their children's view of Genesis 1 is foundational.

And any Sunday service that allows dialogue instead of traditional pulpit preaching is "compromising the message of salvation," as one pastor told me.

However, these are just caricatures of the real issues. The specifics are much more important. To find out the specifics, we will have to get more granular than just talking about the problem of "tradition." And this is where we get most uncomfortable.

Meet David Gushee

Few people are as devoted to the deconstructing mind of Christ as Dr. David Gushee, who has been described as "one of America's leading Christian ethicists."[7] I was first exposed to his work in seminary. His book *Kingdom Ethics* (cowritten with Glen Stassen) was mandatory reading for every seminary student I knew. At the time, it seemed progressive to talk about issues of climate and humanitarian rights. Progressive, for me, was to recycle more and not support torture of any kind.

There are many books between *Kingdom Ethics* and *After Evangelicalism*. Dr. Gushee has changed his mind on quite a few issues, and he has received harsh criticism for it. I have always been fascinated with Gushee's commitment to Jesus, the Bible, and a Christianity that is known for its ethic of love. Unlike many of the other people I interviewed, Gushee hasn't left the faith or the church. Not that many evangelicals haven't tried to push him out. He remains unwaveringly committed to helping the deconstructionist reconstruct a biblically sound faith that is founded on the person of Jesus. As we talked, I became aware of just how *dangerous* deconstruction can be viewed by those in the church.

"From 1994 until, I would say, 2014, I was the go-to evangelical ethics guy," Gushee told me. "If there was an obscure Bible College in the middle of nowhere, I was invited to speak at their chapel." Gushee had a column with *Christianity Today* and spoke at schools like Fuller and Wheaton. He was a master at honing in on the specifics of Christianity that needed reform. Gushee told me about writing an article condemning America's use of torture after 9/11. The main pushback he got was from evangelical Christians. As a sign that I was listening and as one who has had similar experiences, I responded, "Of course."

"Yeah, 'of course' . . . I didn't know it would be 'of course' at that moment!" Gushee replied. "I thought evangelicals were defined by their seriousness in following Jesus. How silly of me."

Gushee continued by explaining how a multifaceted Christianity has both hurt and healed him. He never generalized his dissatisfaction with evangelical doctrine and practice. And he never recommended (in writing or in person) that people who are disoriented by Christianity leave the church. Gushee acknowledged that it's a complex relationship between following Jesus and doing so within the twenty-first-century Western church.

"I'm not able, any longer, to accept that the primary evangelical ways of knowing things are adequate for dealing with the world that we live in, or even for following Jesus," he told me.

It's truly a haunting thought.

After reflecting on his involvement in the evangelical community, and then the fallout when he openly affirmed the LGBTQ+ community, Gushee continued:

"What is evangelicalism? Where are the problems that have caused so many millions to flee? Or to be chewed up by it and to leave the faith altogether? And is there a path out of evangelicalism toward following Jesus that maybe can be helpful?"

To that last question, Gushee quickly mentioned that *After Evangelicalism* is a constructive post-evangelical theology and ethic. We talked at length about the specific parts of Christianity that he deconstructed in his search for Christ.

"Jesus remains the central, non-negotiable figure," he said. "I can confess the Nicene Creed. I can affirm every element of it." Then he started to get specific: "You notice things like the inerrancy of Scripture are not creedal. Right? They were later developments. So the Bible can be central without us having to have a doctrine called inerrancy or infallibility. Central role for Scripture, yes. Inerrancy, no."

With that final statement, I witnessed someone deconstruct a specific topic, and reconstruct it, with seamless confidence. As a leading Christian ethicist, Dr. Gushee has undoubtedly made such statements before. And whether you agree with him or not is beside the point. His interview made it clear that evangelicalism isn't an overwhelmingly helpful brand of Christianity—and for the sake of Jesus, it has to be scrutinized by engaging one specific issue at a time. Gushee continued his critical admiration:

"A lot of the things that people get stuck on in evangelical subcultures really have nothing to do with the non-negotiables of the Christian faith." That last statement summarizes this entire chapter. Perhaps the entire book. He went on to discuss what those subcultures are. From evangelicalism's political alignment with the conservative right to its embrace of xenophobia over other moral commitments, two things were crystal clear. First, the doctrine of Jesus and the historical rootedness of the Christian faith should be of great importance to us. (By historical, I mean getting as close to the original apostles and disciples of Jesus as we can. I do not mean repeated tradition because the church has always done it a certain way.) Second, hitching ourselves to anything other than Jesus and the historical church will cause a catastrophic collision for millions on their journey toward truth. The fact is, we've never seen a traffic jam like this.

We are stuck indeed.

But we don't have to stay here.

Stopping Telling the Truth

A reformation is not born out of new discoveries. That's called a cult. A reformation is born out of rediscovering old truths.

The old truth that seems to get lost so easily is the person and work of Jesus as our clearest revelation of God. What, if any, objection do people have to a loving God dying on the cross for his enemies? Not one of my conversation partners thought that God would be better represented by someone other than Jesus. Furthermore, the death and resurrection of Jesus were among the greatest acts of hope and love for Christians and non-Christians alike. Though they aren't all as articulate about their faith as Dr. Gushee, many of those who are seriously skeptical share his sentiment. Gushee arrived at the conviction that Jesus' authority, as made known in the Gospels, is the cornerstone confession on which every theological house must be built. Lest we think this is too generous of an orthodoxy, the apostle Paul shared this opinion:

> Now I would remind you, brothers, of the gospel I preached to you, which you received, in which you stand, and by which you are being saved, if you hold fast to the word I preached to you— unless you believed in vain. For I delivered to you as of first importance what I also received: that Christ died for our sins in accordance with the Scriptures, that he was buried, that he was raised on the third day in accordance with the Scriptures, and that he appeared to Cephas, then to the twelve.
> 1 CORINTHIANS 15:1-5, ESV

Prior to his conversion, the apostle Paul was a man of tradition. Up until his encounter with Jesus, he was more committed to what he had learned from religion than who God was through Jesus. It's not even that none of Paul's religion was true. It just wasn't built on the right foundation. Yes, the gospel of Jesus is more important than tradition. But in 1 Corinthians 15, we're reminded that the gospel is different, and of greater importance, than other truths. In our attempt to help those who are struggling and falling away from the faith, we try to give them the truth about whatever specific idea is holding them back. *If they don't think like me in this area*, we tell ourselves, *then they aren't a true believer*. Without a foundation of Jesus, a house of truth will eventually crumble.

In his book *One Gospel for all Nations*, Jackson Wu says, "It is possible to compromise the gospel by settling for truth."[8] The gospel is deep enough for all theologians to never reach the bottom and shallow enough for the skeptic to never drown. I say we stop majoring on the minors and let both, tradition and truth, take a backseat to the Good News of Jesus.

Whatever specific truth the deconstructionist is hung up on is substantially less important than the truth about the One who was hung up for them.

In order to help people see this, we must be willing to get to the heart of their issue. Asking *What does Jesus say about the specific idea in question?* is the first step in deconstructing faith so it looks like hope again.

Chapter 7

U: Understand Where It Came From

I didn't go to religion to make me happy. I always knew a bottle of Port would do that. If you want a religion to make you feel really comfortable, I certainly don't recommend Christianity.

C. S. LEWIS

Oh yes, the past can hurt. But the way I see it, you can either run from it or learn from it.

RAFIKI IN *THE LION KING*

MY WIFE, LISA, AND I WERE SITTING across the table from our kids. We were in heavy negotiations with them. We had decided not to eat dinner at the house that night, and we wanted to take them somewhere without toys in the kid's meal. We won every rock, paper, scissors game. They were losing negotiating power from the lack of chores done recently. And then it occurred to me: *Wait—we are the parents!*

"Get in the car, kids. We're going to Red Lobster." I know. I'm such a mean dad.

A Lobster Tale

Lobster isn't a weekly dinner dish at the Ulmer house. It's expensive, my kids are afraid of expanding their palate, and we live in Missouri. The closest native creature we have to the lobster is a turtle. Snapping turtle, to be exact. When we go out for lobster, it is a big deal. This is probably the case with most families, but it hasn't always been that way. Believe it or not, lobster used to be among the most undesirable foods there was. It was seen as a bottom-feeder. The "cockroach of the sea."[1] In 1876, author John J. Rowan wrote, "Lobster shells about a house are looked upon as signs of poverty and degradation."[2] I don't know of a time I saw lobster shells around a house, but I would find it impressive if I ever did! When you and I think of a lobster, it's wearing a top hat and a monocle. Back then, it would have been wearing a baseball cap and tennis shoes.[3]

Don't tell my kids, but maybe their intuition about lobster is right.

In the 1600s, lobsters would wash up on the shore of Massachusetts in two-foot-high piles.[4] The abundance of lobster was embarrassing for the locals. With great hesitation, they fed guests lobster out of necessity. Never out of pride. The very word comes from the Old English *loppe*, which means spider.[5] Is there anything less appetizing than eating an aquatic tarantula? Even through the 1900s, lobster meat wasn't revered as anything special. It used to be sold in a can for 11 cents, sitting on the shelf next to the baked beans for 53 cents.[6] In fact, lobster used to be given to the poor and the prisoner. You get the point.

What is a delicacy today was once considered repulsive and unwanted. So when did lobsters climb the social ladder? When railways started to spread through the states.

Transportation managers figured out a genius way to save money. People who didn't live on the coast had no idea what a lobster was. If they told inlanders the item was rare, exotic, and a symbol of status, they wouldn't know the difference. Chefs started to catch on as they figured out ways to make lobster look more appetizing. Word spread quickly and, before you knew it, lobster was being asked for on salads, in soups, and by the pound.[7] So the next time you're eating a cockroach of the sea, ask yourself, *Is this actually tastier than salmon? Or have I been conditioned to order it on special occasions?* I might have just saved you money!

Over time, social conditioning influenced what people were willing to consume. The further back in history you go, the less appealing lobster was. According to research by France Bellisle for the European Food Information Council:

> Social influences on food intake refer to the impact that one or more persons have on the eating behavior of others, either direct (buying food) or indirect (learn from peer's behavior), either conscious (transfer of beliefs) or subconscious. Even when eating alone, food choice is influenced by social factors because attitudes and habits develop through the interaction with others.[8]

I may have just ruined lobster for you.

When you know the history behind something, it can determine whether you take part in it moving forward. This is true with the Christian tradition as well. The further back in the history of the church you go, the more you realize that certain dogmas and practices common today would have been considered highly undesirable in previous eras. Undoubtedly, we have made a delicacy of many things the church fathers would have—so to say—thrown back into the sea. That is, perhaps, one of the greatest confessions we could offer to the world.

In this chapter, we'll discuss how to review beliefs and practices so that we can understand where they came from. This is a central discipline to the deconstructing mind: not accepting something because "that's how it's always been." So is not rejecting something because "that's how it's always been"! The real Christlike characteristic of a deconstructionist is being able to understand where Christianity came from and how we Christ followers should move forward from here. It's a new way of thinking for evangelicals. As evangelical author and speaker Os Guinness has observed:

> Evangelicals have been deeply sinful in being anti-intellectual ever since the 1820s and 1830s. For the longest time we didn't pay the cultural price for that because we had the numbers, the social zeal, and the spiritual passion for the gospel.[9]

Jesus Knew Better Than the Pharisees

Let's revisit Mark 7, which I touched on in the last chapter. Jesus was being approached by some Pharisees and scribes because they weren't happy with how his followers were acting. His disciples weren't washing their hands before eating. This had nothing to do with hygiene. It was another Jewish custom passed down through oral tradition, and breaking the oral law was equal to breaking God's law in the Pharisees' eyes. Jesus called them out on the ludicrousness of equating human laws with God's law by calling them hypocrites, then quoting a rebuke from the book of Isaiah. The line we finished the story with in the last chapter was Jesus' mic drop moment:

"You have let go of the commands of God and are holding on to human traditions" (Mark 7:8).

Don't forget that this entire FUSE deconstruction strategy comes from Scripture. Lots of people think deconstruction can't have a strategy, while unknowingly following the Jesus template in their own deconstruction.

> [Jesus said,] "You have let go of the commands of God and are holding on to human traditions."
>
> And he continued, "You have a fine way of setting aside the commands of God in order to observe your own traditions! For Moses said, 'Honor your father and mother,' and, 'Anyone who curses their father or mother is to be put to death.' But you say that if anyone declares that what might have been used to help their father or mother is Corban (that is, devoted to God)—then you no longer let them do anything for their father or mother. Thus you nullify the word of God by your tradition that you have handed down. And you do many things like that."
>
> MARK 7:8-13

The word *Corban* is a Greek translation of a Jewish tradition. Scholars aren't quite sure when it was established, but the tradition was passed down orally. Corban was the action of dedicating something to the Lord so it couldn't be taken from the individual. People who did this didn't have to give the item to a priest, neighbor, or even a needy parent.[10] I'm reminded of the scene in *The Office* when Michael Scott starts declaring bankruptcy, thinking that declaring it loudly is all it takes to make it official.[11] As far as we can tell, Corban was similar but for much more selfish reasons.

What is the most valuable item you own? Imagine declaring that you have dedicated it to the Lord. From that point forward, no one could tell you to sell it, trade it, or put it in your will. It would become untouchable. That's Corban. This tradition nullified the word of God to take care of your mother and father (Deuteronomy 27:16), your neighbor (Ecclesiastes 4:10), and the poor and needy (Zechariah 7:9-10). It's obvious that Jesus knew where the tradition came from. By acknowledging that it came from human, not divine, authority, he disarmed the judgment and condemnation brought on his disciples. Jesus did this elsewhere when he was asked about taxes, the Sabbath, or even how people should pray. In all these accounts, Christ's response is aligned with the spiritual posture we find elsewhere in the New Testament. It's a response that elevates the spirit of the law over the law itself.

Romans 8:2 says, "Because you belong to him, the power of the life-giving Spirit has freed you from the power of sin that leads to death" (NLT). This is a major part of everyone's deconstruction journey. When people move away from dogma and legalism and toward love, acceptance, and grace, they are seen as a threat by the evangelical church. But these people are leaning into the spirit of the law, not the law itself. Which makes me wonder: Is it better to obey the letter of the law or to strive to live by the spirit of the law?

In the interviews I conducted for this book, all the former believers that I talked with felt a deep sense of sorrow around the effects of doctrine. The spirit of the law had gotten lost in the letter of the law. The exact wording, literally applied, had become more important than the reason it was written to others in the church, which ended up hurting their brothers and sisters in Christ. Once we understand where ideas and beliefs have come from, we must also ask ourselves why they have been put in place in the first place. If our beliefs don't align with the character of God, should we be passing them down as true Christianity? The character of God, made known in Jesus, should be the filter for all law, tradition, and Christian belief. I believe that understanding why something was written is more foundational than blindly obeying the surface-level interpretation of the letter of the law. A lot of emotions accompany this sort of Christian prioritization. It's a constant back and forth between the pains of denial and the pleasures of discovery. It seems like Jesus did this to his followers regularly.

In the Sermon on the Mount, we encounter the letter of the law rewritten in light of the spirit of the law. It starts with an invitation to those whose spirits are in union with the character of Christ: the poor in spirit (Matthew 5:3), those who are mourning (5:4), the meek (5:5), those wanting justice (5:6), the merciful (5:7), the pure in heart (5:8), the peacemakers (5:9), and the devoted (5:10). It's evident from this message that *the spiritual posture of a believer is more important than their devotion to any given position.* It's such an outlandish sermon opener that Jesus reassures his hearers that he did not come to abolish the law but to fulfill it. "Do not think that I have come to abolish the Law or the Prophets; I have not come to abolish them but to fulfill them" (Matthew 5:17, ESV). Just because Jesus fulfilled the letter of the law doesn't mean that it must be unwaveringly obeyed. Jesus himself healed on the Sabbath, touched the unclean, and performed more scandalous acts than are recounted in the Gospels. Fulfilling the law means honoring the spirit, the reason for which it was established in the first place. To quote theologian Stanley Hauerwas, "The basis for the ethics for the Sermon on the Mount is not what works but rather the way God is."[12]

Before we write all this off as heresy, remember that the rest of Jesus' sermon has to do with getting back to the heart behind obedience. Murder, adultery, divorce, oaths, and a love for our enemies were all rewritten in light of a person's motivation. The more I study Jesus, the more offensive he becomes to my rule-setting—and rule-following—spirit. I try to follow the rules because that is what a good Christian does. Perhaps this is why deconstruction is such an important part of any Christ follower's journey. Deconstruction helps us leave the "good Christian" role so that we can show up in the world as an authentic thinker and wrestler with God.

Three Important Questions

The deconstructing mind asks three important questions before committing to the course. Just as important as *what it says* is *where it comes from* and *why it is there*. Asking these questions now could create a new cultural norm for the next generation. In some cases, these are the questions Gen Z is intuitively asking. These three questions seem to be the logic of Jesus in Mark 7:

- Where does this belief come from?
- Who is it benefiting?
- Who does it harm?

1. Where does this belief come from?

As Christians, when we ask, *Where does this belief come from?*, we are exposing ourselves to the reality that many beliefs that we hold may not be rooted in Scripture or even church history. Even those two criteria feel problematic when we realize that all Scripture is interpreted through a person and all people have tribes and biases they subscribe to. Nevertheless, based on the last chapter, it is truly the words of Jesus we are after. When we ask, *Where does this belief come from?*, we want to know if it is directly from Jesus, or if it sounds like something he would say based on what we know of him from the Scriptures. To this point, I often tell people that I don't believe in Jesus because I believe in the Bible. I believe in the Bible because I believe in Jesus. One can wrestle with entire creeds and doctrines while faithfully following Jesus. Jesus isn't the ABCs of religion; he is the A through Z. Another way of asking this question is: *What does Jesus have to say about this specific topic?*

Fair warning—this will create tension within you. What you find out will oftentimes require repentance on your part.

Yes, that's right.

The Christian must be willing to repent to the skeptic if the two of them are legitimately unearthing problematic beliefs and practices. We must be willing to follow Jesus out of religion. This is part of that path.

2. Who is it benefiting?

This question will challenge the American dream. When we ask this question, we are taking our self-interest out of the equation. It's an incredibly important question to ask yourself, particularly if you are used to living in the shadow of Western evangelicalism. Since Jesus' authority is the agreed on standard for belief and practice, we must remember how he spoke of oppression and the oppressed. "The Spirit of the Lord is upon me, because he has anointed me to proclaim good news to the poor. He has sent me to proclaim liberty to the captives and recovering of sight to the blind, to set at liberty those who are oppressed, to proclaim the year of the Lord's favor" (Luke 4:18-19, ESV). Simply put, if the belief or practice in question doesn't benefit those who are poor (in spirit and/or in flesh) then, by default, it must be benefiting another group. Who is that group? Or more importantly, are we that group and is that why we can't let go?

The question of money seems to come up often when people are deconstructing parts of Christianity. To be more specific, the tax-exempt status of churches. Many people deconstructing this topic wonder why the church can operate like a business but never have to pay taxes. When some churches are bringing in hundreds of millions of dollars a year, setting salaries based on growth metrics, giving bonuses to staff, and doing it all based on the biblical mandate of tithing, it's important we ask, *Who is it benefiting?*

I talked with my friend Bishop Walter Harvey on this issue. Bishop Harvey serves as the CEO of Prism Economic Development Corporation and board president for the National Black Fellowship of the Assemblies of God. His perspective, as a black man, on the tax-exempt status of all churches was enlightening, to say the least. During the election of 2020, Christians were concerned that placing the "wrong" candidate in office would affect the tax exemption that churches and Christian universities enjoy. Some even went so far as to call it persecution. Bishop Harvey had a hard time seeing through the eyes of the evangelical as he answered both questions for me: *Where does this belief come from?* and *Who is it benefiting?*

Harvey explained to me that the 501(c) status originated in 1954 during the rise of the civil rights era. Although exceptions have been made since 1894, it wasn't until 1954 that the modern tax code was established for religious organizations to be exempt from taxes as long as they were limited in their political activities.[13] In 1934 there were limitations set on lobbying activities, but in 1954 the limitations were set on speaking out on whatever topics were deemed "political."[14] Simply put, the 501(c) status was put in place to benefit the white evangelical segregationists in power. It was hush money. Black pastors who were speaking out on issues of racial injustice could gain a tax-exempt status if they stopped speaking out. Do you see why it's important we ask the question *Who is benefiting?*

Despite evangelicals' frequent claims that the Bible is
the source of their social and political commitments,
evangelicalism must be seen as a cultural and political
movement rather than as a community defined chiefly by its
theology.[15]

3. Who does it harm?

It may feel like a subtle shift from the second question, *who is it benefiting*, but let me assure you that this is anything but splitting hairs. With question number two, we are becoming aware of ourselves as we humbly admit that we may be the beneficiaries of any particular idea or belief. By asking *who does it harm,* we are waking up to the reality that we are not only receiving the benefit, but we are possibly participating in harming people in the process.

One of the easiest examples that comes to mind is the doctrine that women aren't permitted to teach men. In this view, women are supposed to submit to a man's authority. Without getting into the crude misuses and abuses of those who have been spiritually wounded by this, it's easy to know who is getting harmed in the process—the 49.6 percent of the world's population that is female. As the father of two daughters, I can't imagine teaching them that the first eyewitnesses to Jesus' resurrection were women, but they aren't allowed to teach in modern-day pulpit ministries. If Jesus based the entire testimony of his resurrection on the witness of a woman, why can't we let a woman speak about the testimony of Christ from the pulpit?

That's not even to mention the harm that comes to a household when a woman is taught to submit to a man's authority based on the sheer fact that he is male. Unfortunately, the horror stories you and I have heard around this doctrine result in a generation being catapulted away from the church. If you grew up watching a man embezzle his authority for personal gain, how likely are you to trust the authority of the God-man, Jesus Christ?

Welcome to the Process

Our family has known Jessica for close to seven years now. Jessica is a therapist who specializes in trauma. She is sought out by many clients for help with spiritual trauma, and she oversees the Instagram account *Welcome to the Process*.[16]

When we planted a church in Denver, Jessica was the first person to move from Texas and join our team. She was a host at the first Doubters' Club meeting, church service, and all our prayer meetings leading up to those events. Jessica spent much of her formative years in a Bible college and serving at churches. She knows what the Bible says. She knows how to be a Christian. And she knows how to deconstruct both.

We hadn't talked in years, but I knew this book felt incomplete without her voice. After a brief exchange of "How are the kids?" and "How is life treating you?" we jumped into her deconstruction journey.

Here was Jessica's response when I asked her what deconstruction is: "Deconstruction is about taking apart your beliefs piece by piece. I do this by asking myself questions like *Where did my beliefs come from? Who do they benefit?* and *Who do they harm? Honestly, is this doing more good than harm?* Letting yourself look at everything upside down is important."

She talked a bit about specific beliefs that have gone through that sort of cross-examination. Then, she made a statement that I know to be true for many of my other interviewees.

"People wouldn't consider me Christian anymore, even though I still have Jesus. That's fine, I guess. I'm living according to my values and my faith in Jesus."

Jessica's values have always revolved around the health and well-being of others. When she first moved to Denver, she worked as a live-in nanny to help a family in need of childcare. That's just one example of the many times she's resisted selfish ambitions for the sake of others.

"What caused your deconstruction, Jess?" I asked.

"I don't think it was a single thing. The church is my safe haven, and it never hurt me like it has so many others. I can think back to middle school and having friends who were gay. I remember being told they are going to hell. Even from a young age, I was trying to figure out where the Bible said gay people were going to hell. Recently, the way evangelicals responded to Trump definitely caused me to give Christianity some distance."

Notice a few things about her response. First, she named the specifics. In this case, the treatment of homosexuals and the affirmation of Donald Trump. Then, she tried to identify where these ideas and beliefs came from. Whether by instinct or a developed impulse, she knew that what was being done (the letter of the law) didn't line up with the spirit of the law (her values). Although it's uncomfortable, it's time we understand *why things are the way they are.* American cultural critic Laura Kipnis is right: "Emotional discomfort is [now] regarded as equivalent to material injury, and all injuries have to be remediated."[17]

This process of investigating and understanding is incredibly vital to the authenticity of someone's deconstruction journey.

Do they need to believe the law is true, or do they need to act out of the spirit of the law?

Repenting from Unbiblical Beliefs

Unfortunately, renewing our minds is truly one of the hardest things we can attempt. In matters of the mind, we have to remember that repentance requires changing our minds on beliefs and practices that we have held on to tightly. And as much as we are tempted to believe repentance is meant for the world and not the church, Jesus aims this word at the religious more than the irreligious. Jesus knows that an unrepentant religion is a harmful, ineffective one. According to most of my interviews, here are the top three reasons the church refuses to see which beliefs are unbiblical:

1. Christians don't see the world as it is. Instead, we see the world through our biased worldview.

Our upbringing.

Our stories.

What worked for us.

These are all crucial to how we show up in the world. One of the most powerful action steps you can take after reading this book is going to your deconstructing friend or family member and admitting that you see the world through a "me lens." If most people experience you as the type of Christian who is certain about their beliefs, this confession would be refreshing, to say the least. It would give the person you were talking with the freedom to become curious, once again, with you. And curious about you.

As I write these words, my daughters are still young enough to think that Lisa and I are the greatest people in the world. Nine and seven are such sweet ages. When they grow up, I fully anticipate visiting them and helping them with their kids, if they have them, I'm also expecting there to be different house rules. When my daughters are adults, I will be at their house with their rules. Maybe they will have a rule that the kids have to go to bed by 8:00 p.m. Or maybe we won't be allowed to talk about politics. Whatever it is, it will be their house. I will need to abide by their rules. It does no good to be rigid about my stance on a whole slew of topics.

The same is true when talking to people about the world. We can't see ourselves as the mediators of truth. We are trying to help people get to God's house. And the rules in God's house are different. They start and end with the authority of Jesus, the One who is Love. His house rules involve understanding why something is the way it is. To help people see the world through our bias creates an unnecessary barrier. Plus, those are the house rules. We must strive to see the world as it is. Namely, loved by God and redeemed by Christ. Any rule we have that doesn't submit to the loving nature of Christ doesn't belong in the house of God.

2. Christians are uncomfortable with how deconstructionists make us feel.

I have a hunch that the Holy Spirit is called the Great Comforter (John 16:7) because we were not meant to live in comfort. Perhaps this is why Jesus seemed to always feel comfortable in his own skin. He was filled with the Spirit, walked in an unshakable identity, and never seemed to be uncomfortable in any situation. Whether sitting with the gluttons and the drunkards or waiting to be executed, Jesus never showed up in the world as uncomfortable. We, on the other hand, are all train wrecks just waiting to happen.

We hold tightly to traditions and practices because they are all we have known. To try anything else is to experience extreme discomfort, and who wants to intentionally step into that? I know pastors who won't attend weddings because there is dancing, and I know dancers who won't attend churches because there is preaching. The difference is one of those groups says to submit to the law of love.

If the actions and viewpoints of a group of people make you uncomfortable but you claim to be a Christian, you are in good company. The Holy Spirit is available to bring you comfort. I believe the Spirit of God is the spirit behind the law. It is the Spirit of God who will deliver us from condemnation, people phobia, and a legalistic mindset that keeps the other out.

3. We don't think other perspectives could have the truth. We think only Christians can hold the truth on issues of morality.

Embracing someone else's view can be an excruciating process. Especially when that someone else is not the type of Christian that you are. Or they are younger than you. Or older. It requires two intolerable confessions: I was wrong, and you are right. Then there is the added complexity of the spirit of the law. Even if you are right, but they are acting more like Jesus, whose actions are more acceptable in God's eyes?

> To some who were confident of their own righteousness and looked down on everyone else, Jesus told this parable: "Two men went up to the temple to pray, one a Pharisee and the other a tax collector. The Pharisee stood by himself and prayed: 'God, I thank you that I am not like other people—robbers, evildoers, adulterers—or even like this tax collector. I fast twice a week and give a tenth of all I get.'
>
> "But the tax collector stood at a distance. He would not even look up to heaven, but beat his breast and said, 'God, have mercy on me, a sinner.'
>
> "I tell you that this man, rather than the other, went home justified before God. For all those who exalt themselves will be humbled, and those who humble themselves will be exalted."
>
> LUKE 18:9-14

This point reminds me of C. S. Lewis's character Ransom in his book *Out of the Silent Planet*. Ransom planned on taking a year-long sabbatical from teaching at Cambridge but is abducted and put on a spaceship on its way to Malacandra (Lewis's reimagining of Mars). Ransom is the intended sacrifice to the Malacandrian creatures (called sorns). He is surprised to find this monthlong journey a spiritual awakening of sorts. Instead of doom and darkness, his experiences resemble markings of the heavens. It's a lengthy and wordy book, but it's worth rereading until you get it. Ransom's fear of space is much like many Christians' fear of deconstruction.

We Are All Mad

I was speaking at a church in Seattle on faith and doubt. I hadn't preached there before, but I could tell it was a mixed crowd. Some people were leaning in while others were ready to leave. One lady was bouncing her leg and taking notes at the same time. A confusing combination for sure. Finding me immediately after the service, she asked, "Do you have any Doubters' Clubs in Arkansas? Please tell me you do!"

"I'm sorry," I told her. "I don't think we do. I'll double-check when I get to my computer."

"My son lives there, and he is a doubter." By that, she meant he was agnostic. It takes a while for people to realize that doubters and Christians are one and the same. "He moved there for college and all of a sudden he started rethinking every single little thing about Christianity. That's his problem. He thinks about where all our beliefs come from."

"Ma'am," I told her, "thinking is a really good thing! It's when we don't think about our beliefs that we get into trouble. Have you tried understanding him?"

"No! I'm not changing my mind," she exclaimed.

I thought to ask her a clarifying question. "Does your son claim to be a Christian?"

"Yes. But he doesn't believe what we believe."

That's when I knew we were dealing with a strong bias, rooted in a certain brand of Christianity.

Here's the lesson I took away from my conversation with this woman: Don't be the first to call someone "unchristian" and the last to investigate your traditions. Learn to love knowledge. As C. S. Lewis wrote, "The love of knowledge is a kind of madness."[18]

Chapter 8

S: Share the Impact

Jesus was not a theologian. He was God who told stories.
QUOTED IN MADELEINE L'ENGLE, *WALKING ON WATER*

*Worse? How could [things] get any worse? Take a look
around you, Ellen. We're at the threshold of hell!*
CLARK GRISWOLD IN *NATIONAL LAMPOON'S CHRISTMAS VACATION*

"DAD, TELL US A STORY!" It's a nightly request from the kids.

I can always read them a story, but they prefer it when I tell them one from when I was their age. Stories about my life introduce my children to a version of Dad they have never met. They want to know what life was like for me when I was their age, or how their mother and I met. I was a risk-taking child who did ollies off rooftops. I punched a bully in high school and never let him hit me back (at least that's how I tell it). I outran a herd of cows that were chasing my dad and me down a hillside. The girls cozy up every night for another episode of *My Dad Was Cooler When He Was a Kid.* I love it!

My kids have laughed and cried at my stories of making and losing friends. It's become a game at bedtime. I tell them a true story about my life and exaggerate a bit. It's Piper and Brennan's job to yell "Exaggeration!" when they hear some outlandish detail. Sometimes they get lost in the grandiosity of my adventures and forget to call me out.

I'll pause for a bit to give them a chance to catch up. Piper will slowly start to smile and glance at Brennan to see if she caught it. Brennan will pop up out of bed, point her finger at me, and yell "Exaggeration!" as if it were her idea. Tonight's story was about my improv drama performance in high school. Improv because I forgot to study and there was a test that day.

"Exaggeration!" Brennan yelled.

"No, honey. I didn't study in high school. Now, go to bed." It wasn't my best night.

Claims of Exaggeration

Looking for the exaggerated facts of a story is a fun bedtime routine, but it's defeating when the church does this to its own people.

Many pastors I know think stories of church hurt are being exaggerated on social media and then broadcasted on podcasts. Which, quite frankly, only perpetuates the problem. What I have found from talking with many nones and dones is that they are *not* exaggerating.

When a Christian tells a story about their church experience, it is valid because it is what they experienced. To assume deconstructionists are elaborating or exaggerating is disrespectful, dismissive, and unacceptable. People have truly experienced harsh realities within Christian community, and they need to be able to talk about it. Within the FUSE strategy for the deconstructing mind, there needs to be room for the Christian and the non-Christian to share what they've learned and how it's affected them. This sharing should involve both what they have studied and their personal experiences.

In her book *Sacred Wandering*, Dana Arcuri gives us a clear picture of how Jesus would let people share their stories:

Jesus would publicly call out people in the faith community who are guilty for hurting/violating others. He wouldn't sit back in silence. He wouldn't bury the evidence. Or cover up abuse. In addition, He would never ignore, condemn, or ostracize those who've suffered trauma. He wouldn't say, "*Get over it.*"[1]

Jesus wouldn't say, "Get over it" because he couldn't get over *them*. Those who were violated and silenced by the religious leaders were validated and sacred to Jesus.

Why Chatty Chad Left Christianity

Chad doesn't have the ability to overlook anyone who crosses his path. He works two jobs, both in customer service. During the morning, he works in sales, while his afternoons are filled with valet parking some of the nicest vehicles in town. Chad has some far-fetched stories of how customers have treated him. But he prefers to talk about the nice cars he has driven. Some were so nice that he couldn't find the doorknob to climb in and drive it away. We both laugh as Chad recounts these experiences. But we stop laughing when he talks about religion. I wish I could say those accounts are far-fetched as well, but the reality is Chad is still holding back some of the details.

Growing up in rural America is an essential aspect of Chad's childhood. He almost blamed his deconversion on it. His family was thoroughly evangelical and volunteered in the church. The blessing and curse of living in a small town is that everyone knows you—which means everyone knows your business. They have expectations about who you will be when you grow up, how you will handle the family business, and what type of girl you are going to marry. All false prophecies as far as Chad was concerned.

"I didn't hang out with a lot of the folks around town," he told me. "They were small-minded, and they laughed at the type of people I wished I had in my life. I wanted to be friends with people who helped communities. People who made a difference with their lives." He sipped his coffee while on the verge of laughing as he told me stories about his upbringing. One of the baristas interrupted us to say hello. Everyone knew Chad because Chad had a desire to know everyone.

"Can I ask you something?" I said as we got back to our conversation.

"Sure. What's up?"

"What made you deconstruct your Christianity?" I asked.

For the first time, there was no smirk or smile on his face. Here was Chad's response:

"That's just it. It was never my Christianity. But I suppose the thing that did it for me was my experience. My story wasn't well received by the pastors and church members. When I was in high school, I went to the principal and told him I wanted to bring a guy with me to prom. The principal wouldn't allow it. I let him know that I was gay. I thought if he put himself in my shoes for a second . . . and this next part really pissed me off. The principal looked at me and said, 'That's your problem, Chad. Just stop being gay!'"

As bad as that is, it still wasn't the worst part. I wish the next detail were an exaggeration.

"All the churches in my town were so small that the pastors often had to find work outside of the church. My principal was also my pastor. Do you know how it feels to be told that being attracted to guys is my problem? Two years later, it came out that my pastor had an affair."

I had no words to respond to Chad. How do you defend Christianity when the Christians in the story look more like twisted hypocrites than their affectionate, come-as-you-are God? Chad's story might have proved Hindu philosopher Swami Vivekananda right when he said, "It is better to be an outspoken atheist than a hypocrite."[2] Once Chad graduated high school, he moved to the East Coast for two years. He didn't find the answers he needed, so he went to the West Coast for a while. His goal was to study and find answers to life's questions. The church didn't seem to do a good job at that. Or, as they say in the movies, he had to "Get outta dodge!" I told him he reminded me of Dr. Strange from the Marvel movie of that name. After an injury, Stephen Strange goes on a global quest to find healing for his body and soul. The healing he needed was a spiritual awakening that would end up becoming his superpower. His healing would eventually heal the world. Finally, Chad was laughing again.

"I will never be interested in calling myself a Christian again, Preston."

I nodded. "Forget calling yourself a Christian. What did you learn about Jesus? Outside of religion, was learning about him helpful to you?"

"That's interesting," he said. "When I learned about Jesus, I was at peace. Who I learned about him from is where I became suspicious."

Bingo.

That last phrase was the key to unlocking an age-old principle about sharing our faith with skeptics. When church hurt is involved, we have to build trust before we can present Jesus as trustworthy. That is why allowing space to share the impact of our stories is critical to the process.

Talking about religious trauma and spiritual abuse usually requires the scars to show you have been through it. Few within the church have earned the right to speak on the issue. So we defend ourselves instead. Or worse, we defend the abuser, who we don't even know. Just because they claim to be a Christian. I don't know about you, but sometimes it's difficult calling myself a Christian. Not because I'm ashamed of Jesus. On the contrary! It's because I am concerned that the word *Christian* doesn't properly represent the Jesus I believe overturned religious abuse. We have to be willing to listen to the Chads of the world if we are going to redeem the deconstructionist movement. Sharing the impact of what we have learned—and what we have lived—is the key to building the trust it takes to pioneer the path of uncertainty together.

Sharing our stories requires conversation, and conversations require listening. Listening is the number one way we gain trust, and trust is required for there to be any sort of bridge between someone's current story and the chapters not yet written. According to Judith Glaser in *Conversational Intelligence*, our brains are wired so they require sharing stories to move us from distrust to trust.[3] This is a leap of intentionality that the church owes the world.

The Importance of Trust

Have you ever had a conversation with a doubter where all you could think about was how wrong they were?

Or perhaps all you could think about was how you were going to respond.

The way forward between Christians and doubters is not suspicion.

Trust is what is missing in almost every conversation between a Christian and a non-Christian. To build trust, you have to have conversations (yes, plural) where you listen more than you talk. Conversations are like threads, albeit fragile ones, that keep our stories connected to the person on the other side of the table. But we are only as connected as the other person is willing to listen. According to Glaser, conversations are not merely an exchange of ideas or emotions. Conversations are the vehicles of our stories, and they create realities, perspectives, even new paradigms: "They evolve and impact the way we connect, engage, interact, and influence others, enabling us to shape reality, mind-sets, events, and outcomes in a collaborative way."[4] Conversations are the highways that our stories travel on to get from one heart to another. And when a story reaches a heart, it is either transformed by it or it does the transforming. Either way, transformation is happening. New perspectives are being had. Emotions are being felt. Loneliness is disappearing. Jesus' presence is being made known.

All this rhetoric about the intricacies of dialogue seems pointless unless you realize that there is truly no other way to continue the deconstruction journey until you are willing to gain trust with the doubter.

Our brains are wired to allow people to influence us as they earn our trust. On one side of the brain, you have the amygdala. This is the primitive part of the brain that pumps stress hormones into your body. It's commonly referred to as the "fight or flight" part. Anytime your body senses danger, the amygdala is triggered. It's not the part of the brain that comes up with clever lies to get you out of trouble but the part that tells you that you need to come up with a lie. "On the other side of the brain is the prefrontal cortex." As Glaser explains, this "enables us to build societies, have good judgment, be strategic, handle difficult conversations, and build and sustain trust."[5] Think of it like this: If you're somewhere you haven't been before and you hear a rustle in the bushes, your amygdala will tell you that it's a predator and you need to run for the hills. If you know the territory, however, your prefrontal cortex will reason quickly that there are no predators around and you can explore the sound more. You become curious where you used to become cautious. Similarly, when talking with people about what they are learning and what they have experienced, we have to know the territory—a lot better than we do.

Judith Glaser goes even further by categorizing different parts of the brain to help us see when we are triggered. In order to prevent ourselves from going into "lockdown" mode and getting stuck on our point of view, it's important that we realize the value of listening. It can change how the brain responds to someone who thinks differently than we do. Notice the different groupings in the diagram on the next page. According to Glaser, our amygdala is the low trust part of our brain. Also grouped in the low-trust area are the characteristics of resistor and skeptic. In the middle of our brains is the conditional-trust category. Grouped in conditional trust is a more active characteristic: wait and see. As we discussed earlier, the front of our brains is high trust. This is where two incredible actions are taking place. When trust is high, people are willing to experiment and co-create to engage the world around them. So the major question is: How do we go from resistor to co-creator? As the diagram points out, this is done through listening.[6]

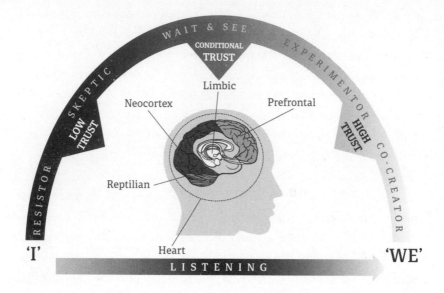

Let me anticipate an objection. You may be thinking, *What if we do all the listening and trusting, but they stay resistant to continuing the conversation?* One more science lesson is in order. Have you ever heard of the effect of mirroring?

Mirroring is the subconscious action of copying someone's gestures or posture, and this only takes place when someone is starting to feel the emotions of another person's story. Remember when your mom told you not to stand there with your arms crossed when you're in conversation? This is why! If you look like you are closed off, others will become closed off to you. Leading neurologist Marco Iacoboni attributes neurological tendencies of mirroring to what he calls "mirror neurons" or "smart cells."[7] The gesture of listening mirrors how we hope someone will listen to us. More than that, it gives us the gift of empathy. I don't think the question is why doubters and skeptics aren't listening to Christians anymore. Science has given us the answer, and the Bible has given us the example.

The reason the deconstructing mind hasn't trusted the church is because the church hasn't modeled a listening posture.

I love it when the Bible shows off when science shows up.

Jesus Practiced Mirroring

As we have seen in previous chapters, Mark 7 is one of the greatest texts when it comes to deconstruction. It is a remarkable account of Jesus modeling the original template. Let's continue with verses 14-15:

> Again Jesus called the crowd to him and said, "Listen to me, everyone, and understand this. Nothing outside a person can defile them by going into them. Rather, it is what comes out of a person that defiles them."
> MARK 7:14-15

There it is. That pesky, passive word that makes us feel like we aren't accomplishing much: *listen*. Following his exchange with the Pharisees, Christ now turns to the crowd, telling them to listen. He was about to share with them the effects that tradition has had, but it was most important that they first listen. What was happening to people's frame of mind when they chose to listen to Jesus stand up for them?

I imagine the resistors in earshot of his voice were willing to wait and see how the dialogue panned out. Perhaps those who were already waiting and seeing were now willing to experiment by trusting in what Jesus had to say. I can imagine a Jew making the liberating choice to eat with unwashed hands. It was a new way of living. No longer did the Pharisees get to pass on their senseless traditions to those they were unwilling to listen to. Now, there was a new person to trust.

As crowds followed Jesus, they watched the religious become unhinged at his critiques. As they talked to him, they became braver in personally connecting to God, a practice that wasn't allowed before.

And as they listened to Jesus, they began to trust that he might be God himself. The face in the mountain they had been looking for all along.

The church is meant to be the body of Christ to the world. We should enchant the deconstructing individual today as Jesus did back then.

A Script for Enchantment

How do we start this conversation around sharing the impact of what we have learned and experienced? I wanted to provide a script for you that would be easy to write on a small sheet of paper or type as a note on your phone. The goal is not to rehearse this script word for word. Use these words as you do a birthday or anniversary card. The questions are meant to give you a starting place, but it's important that you personalize them. One more important reminder before you get started:

You have to go first in the conversation.

By leading with humility, you're admitting that you haven't figured everything out. You are setting the stage for your deconstructing friend to do the same. It's the mirror effect! It's scary to lead the conversation, so let me take the lead. Here are some ways to start sharing the impact:

> Thanks for meeting with me again. A few months ago, you let me know that you were deconstructing your faith. The things you have been deconstructing within Christianity are things that, quite honestly, I have just taken for granted. I haven't thoroughly thought through _____ [*insert the specific topic*]. The things I am learning are challenging, to say the least. Would you mind if I shared those with you? I think there are some key areas where I am changing my mind.

You can't control the other person's response, but I imagine most people will invite you to keep talking. Even if your study hasn't revolutionized your thinking, surely you have learned some new history or stories about the topic you've been studying. But if human tradition is what the deconstructing mind is trying to reimagine, it's likely that we will all end up repenting to some degree. This is where we apologize for our dogmatic approach to a topic. Here is some language for that part of your conversation:

- "I've drawn lines in the sand where they shouldn't have ever been. Please forgive me."
- "I've unknowingly been part of the problem. Please forgive me."
- "I've held on to my interpretation tighter than I have held on to you. Please forgive me."

That last one is especially powerful coming from a parent to a child. Once you've apologized for the impact your view has had on them, wait for their response. Let them respond honestly.

Anger.

Shock.

Tears.

Joy.

All emotions are valid at this point. The temptation is to immediately tell them where your stance hasn't changed and how you still may disagree with them. You will never find a script written by me that starts "Although I think you're wrong . . ." Resist that temptation. The deconstructionist knows your view. That's what got us here in the first place. When you share the impact this journey is having on you, with a humble posture, you are more likely to eventually shift someone's perspective (if that's what you are after). Or they will shift yours. Which may need to happen in certain situations.

With that said, you were never commanded to shift people's perspectives. *Conversion was never the goal.* Disciplemaking was! For you to be a disciplemaker, people have to be willing to follow you, and no one wants to follow a know-it-all. But people *will* follow someone who does the hard work of learning, confessing, and listening. Now for the listening part:

Would you be willing to share the impact _____ [*insert topic*] has had on you? I'm not going to defend anyone or any group of people. I just want to give you the listening ear you need and deserve. In fact, let me turn my phone off. [*Actually turn it off.*]

Would you be willing to share your story with someone if they approached you this way? When you feel tempted to get defensive, let that be a trigger that you need to ask a clarifying question.

Once the conversation has been had, it's time for the final part of lighting the FUSE: Engage with the remains. I'm currently writing in a coffee shop, and five minutes ago I heard glass break. I looked over to see the tip jar in a thousand pieces on the floor! Sitting on top of the shards of glass are the dollar bills from the jar, probably around fifteen dollars total. Even though the whole jar is smashed to smithereens, the things of value remain. Nobody panicked when the container broke. It's what was inside that mattered.

The broken jar and untorn bills remind me of the next chapter.

When a person's faith is shattered, there is Someone who will always remain. Now that we have let go of our tradition, let's engage with him. This is where the real value of Christianity lies.

Chapter 9

E: Engage with the Remains

The more we let God take us over, the more truly ourselves we become—because He made us. He invented us. He invented all the different people that you and I were intended to be. . . . It is when I turn to Christ, when I give up myself to His personality, that I first begin to have a real personality of my own.

C. S. LEWIS, *MERE CHRISTIANITY*

It's not about how much we lost. It's about how much we have left.

TONY STARK IN *AVENGERS: ENDGAME*

IT MAY NOT BE A TRUE STORY, but like parables, they don't need to be true to have an impact. In his book *In the Eye of the Storm*, Max Lucado includes the following story:

> Two battleships assigned to the training squadron had been at sea on maneuvers in heavy weather for several days. I was serving on the lead battleship and was on watch on the bridge as night fell. The visibility was poor with patchy fog, so the captain remained on the bridge keeping an eye on all activities.
>
> Shortly after dark, the lookout on the wing reported, "Light, bearing on the starboard bow."
>
> "Is it steady or moving astern?" the captain called out.
>
> The lookout replied, "Steady, Captain," which meant we were on a dangerous collision course with that ship.

The captain then called to the signalman, "Signal that ship: 'We are on a collision course, advise you change course twenty degrees.'"

Back came the signal, "Advisable for you to change course twenty degrees."

The captain said, "Send: 'I'm a captain, change course twenty degrees.'"

"I'm a seaman second-class," came the reply. "You had better change course twenty degrees."

By that time the captain was furious. He spat out, "Send: 'I'm a battleship. Change course twenty degrees.'"

Back came the flashing light, "I'm a lighthouse."

We changed course.[1]

On a Collision Course

As much as we would like to think we are the lighthouse in the story, we aren't. Jesus is the lighthouse. Both the world and the church have lost their way.

I believe God is giving the church an opportunity to live up to Jesus' words. In order for that to happen, the church must make two commitments.

First, we must adopt a deconstruction mindset that is committed to separating Christian subculture and human tradition from the Kingdom ethics we find in the words of Christ.

Second, we must be willing to change course where needed. If we continue with the lighthouse illustration, perhaps we have already collided. The "us versus them" narrative has increased the polarization between the sacred and the secular. The left and the right. The churched and the unchurched. Churches are doubling down on ways to get the unsaved in the walls of their building; meanwhile, the walls of the building are being deconstructed in the minds of so many. This is why we must approach Jesus with a commitment to both deconstruction *and* reconstruction.

Any book on deconstruction would be incomplete without acknowledging the need for reconstruction. That is, rebuilding the theological house on the words, actions, and beliefs of Jesus. Reconstruction can also be thought of as changing course. As admitting that Jesus is signaling for us to get out of dangerous waters—and then doing something about it. In whatever way you think about reconstruction, the verdict is in: The only way forward is to follow Jesus. To let his authority have the last word. This is good and bad news.

The good news: Simply follow Jesus and let nothing get in the way. He won't just lead us out of an old way but into a new (better) one.

The bad news: Following Jesus is never simple. Especially when religion gets involved.

The Naked Pastor

Interviewing David Haward was a privilege. David is a blogger and runs the Instagram handle @nakedpastor. During our interview, I asked why he decided to use that name.

"I want to be authentic and vulnerable," he told me. He didn't want to post about church growth or becoming a better you. The masquerade of the social-media highlight reel seemed hypocritical. Plus, David was done with church culture. In our interview I learned about his journey through pastoring and how he finds contentment in his current role, helping those who are deconstructing.

In 2010 he finally pushed the envelope too far in the "ministry world" and decided to leave church ministry. His overseers were receiving letters about the questions he was asking. He knew that his propensity toward questioning wasn't going to stop, and he needed to find an exit strategy. Throughout our time, David let me know that he doesn't talk about reconstruction much because he doesn't think you ever stop deconstructing. I listened, sipping my coffee and taking notes. Trying to model what was written about in the last chapter. Not trying to insert where I disagree but trying to unearth his story. The sacred seeds of his education and experience have grown into a unique garden. I was only visiting for an hour. I would rather smell the roses than point out the weeds. And in my listening, I heard a metaphor that I will never forget.

"My deconstruction . . . I compare it to a glacier melt. It took decades of trying to reconcile what I believed with orthodoxy, the Bible, and with the suspicion that there was something more that I was missing."

I'll never forget that line from David. Reconciling what he believed with the suspicion that there is something more out there. A valiant quest for any spiritually aware individual! I imagine there are some reading this book who prefer the term *reconcile* over *reconstruct*. We reconcile our budgets. We reconcile our relationships. Reconciliation is when we want any number of things to coexist in harmony with one another. It's not that I disagree with this; I just don't think it takes us far enough. Living in a constant state of perplexity seems to be rather paralyzing for anyone who wants to make a noticeable difference in the world.

I use my interview with the Naked Pastor in this chapter because I think he is a good example of someone who has deconstructed his faith and reconstructed something new. It isn't that David reconstructed a thoroughly Christian worldview. But the reality is: Everyone who deconstructs will reconstruct some sort of belief. Even to say, "I won't reconstruct a Christian worldview" is a sort of reconstruction. I'm not sure there is a category for David's reconstruction. He doesn't fit into a denomination or a particular brand of Christianity, but that's beside the point. My point is: *Everyone is reconstructing*, even if the reconstruction doesn't look like any theological home you've seen before. My hope in this chapter (and this book) is that you will find the tools you need to reconstruct a Jesus-centered view of your life and the world.

There will always be a tension between our beliefs and the world we live in. It's a tension to manage, not solve. Reconciling our beliefs with

Christianity is a lifelong endeavor that may drive us mad in the end. As author Joan D. Vinge once said, "The contradictions are what make human behavior so maddening and yet so fascinating, all at the same time."[2] Without interviewing the Naked Pastor, I don't think I would have seen this. Even though we view the importance of reconstruction differently, I must agree that any deconstructionist must have an eager longing to reconcile what they believe with the suspicion that there is more out there. Reconciliation is step one for reconstruction, and the first step to reconciliation is admitting where we've gotten it wrong.

That being said, it's not enough to merely admit where we are wrong. To reconstruct, we must be willing to make changes where necessary. This is the irony of it all! As long as we're only admitting where we're wrong, we'll stay in the land of deconstruction. To reconstruct, we have to be willing to change our beliefs and our actions. Faith is a human experience, after all, and it must be formed by our actions.

For the "naked pastors" out there, I'm proud of you for bravely confronting the impoverished spirituality of the West. You might find yourself exposed by the vulnerabilities of your experiences and the inconsistencies of your beliefs, but don't stop at reconciling the two. There is more work to be done. On the other side of perplexity is not certainty but humility. In fact, to be certain about what can't be known is to be what you started running from in the first place. It's fundamentalism of another kind. Deconstruction is the easy part. Who doesn't like lighting the fuse, stepping back, and watching it crumble? The work comes in the honeycombing process. Methodically chipping away at the mountain. Making sure that what we're after isn't ruining the mountain but restoring the face of Jesus. Reconstruction feels dangerous, and it is. We feel exposed because we are. We are an exhausted, daring bunch, aren't we? But there is a difference between being tired of it and tired in it. Being tired *of* Christianity means you're only in it for the explosions. Being tired *in* Christianity means you're committed to the reconstruction process.

Stay in it.

Help us see Jesus in what you're doing.

Don't settle for anything less than rebuilding.

Before continuing in this chapter, I ask that you pause to reflect on some thoughts by Ernest L. Stech. It will help you take one more adventurous step into the discipline of reconstruction.

That's my soul lying there,
You don't know what a soul is?
You think it's some kind of ghostly sheet-like thing you can see through
    and it floats in the air?
That's my soul lying there
Remember when my hand shook because I was nervous in the group?
Remember the night I goofed and argued too much and got mad and
    couldn't get out of the whole mess?
I was putting my soul on the line.
Another time I said that someone once told me something about herself
    that she didn't have to.
I said that she told me something that could have hurt her.
And I guess I was asking you to do the same.
I was asking you to let me know you.
That's part of my soul, too.
When I told you that my mother didn't love my dad and I knew it as
    a kid,
When I said that my eyes water when I get hurt even though I'm
    thirty-four and too much of a man to cry,
I was putting my soul out there in the space between you and me.
Yeah, that's my soul lying there.
I've never met God.
I mean I've never met that old man who sits on a cloud with a crown
    and a staff and knows everything and is everything and
    controls everything.

But I've met you.
Is that God in your face?
Is that God in your soul lying there?
Well, that's my soul lying there.
I'll let you pick it up
That's why I put it there.
It'll bruise and turn rancid like an old banana if you want to
    manhandle it.
It'll go away if you want to ignore it.
But if you want to put your soul there beside it, there may be love.
There may even be God.[3]

Jesus Is a Builder

The same voice that called you to deconstruct is calling you to reform and rebuild. He is calling us all further.

> Everyone then who hears these words of mine and does them
> will be like a wise man who built his house on the rock. And
> the rain fell, and the floods came, and the winds blew and beat
> on that house, but it did not fall, because it had been founded
> on the rock. And everyone who hears these words of mine and
> does not do them will be like a foolish man who built his house
> on the sand. And the rain fell, and the floods came, and the
> winds blew and beat against that house, and it fell, and great
> was the fall of it.
> MATTHEW 7:24-27, ESV

It would be foolish to pursue Jesus out of institutionalized religion and not go any further. Unless, of course, it wasn't Jesus you were after. In which case, telling the church they don't look like Jesus would have been in vain since the authority of Jesus wouldn't matter much anyway.

If you're deconstructing ideas within Christianity that don't seem to line up with the teachings and actions of Jesus, you must keep listening when he tells you to build a theological house. Otherwise, Jesus was just a means to get to the end of you. For Christ wasn't just a carpenter who lived among humans two thousand years ago. Christ is the carpenter who lives among us now. He is the great builder and renovator. To not let him rebuild your faith is to not care about the words of Christ. Does his authority over your spiritual home shock you as much as it shocked his original audience?

> When Jesus finished these sayings, the crowds were astonished at his teaching, for he was teaching them as one who had authority, and not as their scribes.
> MATTHEW 7:28-29, ESV

One can almost substitute "pastors" or "church culture" for "scribes." I, for one, am shocked at the location of this passage. Matthew 7, about rebuilding a house on a solid foundation, follows the Beatitudes in Matthew 5 and the Sermon on the Mount in Matthew 6. Every deconstructionist I know is an advocate for adopting these Kingdom ethics as a universal standard for how we should treat one another. It's a paradigm shift on two incredibly sensitive issues: justice and what type of people are in the Kingdom of Heaven. Not who makes it in. What type of people are *already* in. Of the Beatitudes, Bible scholar Vernon McGee said, "It is well to note that they are be-attitudes, not do-attitudes. They state what the subjects of the kingdom are—they are the type of person described in the Beatitudes."[4] It's the "give me liberty or give me death" speech for those who were tired of religion. And a death sentence for those who were tied to it.

The good news for deconstructionists is that the words of Jesus are what one's new faith needs to look like. We don't need to burden ourselves with rebuilding a brand of Christianity that almost looks like

Jesus. Follow his voice and actions, and you'll have a theology that can withstand any storm.

Sometimes Jesus causes storms to shake us out of the comfort of a world without him. Other times, he calms them. But in all times, he promises to be the foundation that can withstand them with.

As Eugene Peterson put it in *The Message*:

> These words I speak to you are not incidental additions to your life, homeowner improvements to your standard of living. They are foundational words, words to build a life on. If you work these words into your life, you are like a smart carpenter who built his house on solid rock. Rain poured down, the river flooded, a tornado hit—but nothing moved that house. It was fixed to the rock.
>
> MATTHEW 7:24-25, MSG

How to Know If It's Jesus

We can't keep waiting on someone other than Jesus to lead us to a better version of Christianity. This movement was meant to look like him and no one else. When reconstructing a faith that works, there will always be the "scribes" vying for authority over Jesus. Remember, the goal is not to look more Christian (whatever that means). The goal is to look like Jesus and to see the world as he does. Here is a framework to measure all doctrines, actions, and traditions against as we build a faith that looks like our Savior.

1. Hold your assumptions loosely until confirmed by the authority of Christ.

Imagine the freedom you would have if you didn't expect everyone to hold the same preferences as you. The judgment would stop. The anxiety would drop. Who knows . . . maybe the prayer-request list would even shrink.

I occupy a strange space in the church world. I will never abandon the church, but I feel more at home with the doubter. For years, I felt quite lonely in my religious circle, until I found the company of G. K. Chesterton. After reading three Chesterton books in a month, I was tempted to become a Catholic. He taught me that "angels can fly because they can take themselves lightly,"[5] and that we are always supposed to be drawn to, and drawing in, the nonreligious. Anglican theologian David Pickering said of Chesterton:

> He deployed a set of rhetorical devices that enabled him to create common ground with his readers. He used these devices to present himself as a friend, and to claim that he presented religious questions to his readers in the manner of an unbiased explorer, in spite of his own faith commitments. As part of this strategy, he restricted the range of theology he used in his apologetics so as to remain as far as possible within boundaries his non-religious readers could easily relate to.[6]

Have you ever considered restricting the range of your theology for the sake of the nonreligious? This means your smoking friends are allowed to smoke. Your drinking friends are allowed to drink. And your vegan friends are allowed to eat tofu. More seriously, your son is allowed to believe in a different creation account than you. Your parent is allowed to vote more conservatively than you. And your crazy uncle is allowed to be a conspiracy theorist. Think of your family and friends like your portfolio—diversify as much as possible!

As far as I can tell, Jesus was the personification of truth and wisdom. Yet we know nothing about his personal preferences. The only time we see him draw a line in the sand is when religious men are condemning a nonreligious woman caught in the act of adultery. He wasn't drawing in the sand to keep her out but to bring her in! We shouldn't be drawing lines where Jesus welcomed others. Our preferences and biases have historically been a big deal to us. In the words of Christ, "Go and sin no more" (John 8:11, NLT).

2. Don't allow your knee-jerk reactions toward deconstruction to distract you from the reconstruction process.

Not long ago, I was helping a disillusioned woman through the deconstruction process when I received an email from her mother.

> My daughter doesn't believe in the devil anymore. She says you have deconstructed, too! I don't understand how you can love God but not believe in the devil. Are you teaching this? ... And don't you dare tell her I contacted you!

Don't worry; I didn't tell her daughter. I decided to put it in this book instead.

Beyond all the exclamation marks making me feel like I was being yelled at, I was confused by the accusation that I don't believe in the devil. I've never taught that. If you've ever heard me pray, you would know that I believe there is a spiritual warfare at play and that we need God's intervention.

It's interesting when I read a reactionary message like this one. On the one hand, they express concern for the well-being of their loved one. On the other hand, these kinds of reactions will only slingshot their loved one further from Jesus. At one point in our exchange, I felt it was important to let this woman know that "very rarely are people pushed closer to Jesus." Remember in grade school when we learned Newton's third law of motion, for every action, there is an equal and opposite reaction? Our reactions don't just push people further away; they make us more stubborn and set in our ways.

While I was visiting a town in California, a pastor told me that "his congregation is doing just fine without asking questions." I believe his next declaration was: "We have never been smaller than we are right now. But the people who are part of the church are true Christians. At least we don't have doubters in our midst when we pray. The prayers of the righteous will prevail, not the prayers of the doubters." Some days I laugh when I hear such things. Most of the time, it makes me sad. So much growth would happen if more parents and pastors would deconstruct their own faith for the sake of arriving at a more Jesus-centered one.

Instead, too much of their energy is spent taking shots at those who are asking the right questions. The more we react, the less likely we are to research and listen. And if we react, may it be in alignment with Jesus, not the church. Lest we forget that the authority of Jesus—and the image of God that we have in him—is more important than anything else we can fight for.

John Cooper, a musician for Skillet, said in an interview that it's time we declare war on the deconstruction movement. He's afraid that the younger generation has divorced Jesus from the Bible. "There is no such thing as divorcing Jesus Christ from the Bible. That is not a thing," Cooper told a young audience. He continued:

> I don't hate those deconstructed Christians. I pray for their repentance. But listen, they have divorced themselves from God, and they want to take as many of you people as they can. And it is time for us and your generation to declare war on this idolatrous deconstruction Christian movement.[7]

Cooper's reaction to deconstructionism has blinded him from what is actually taking place. It sounds noble, but it's a sloppy caricature of what's actually happening. The deconstruction movement is trying to decipher (a more accurate verb) Jesus from unhealthy, and unhelpful, interpretations of the Bible. Something that devoted Jesus followers have practiced since they started following him.

3. Have a high tolerance for paradoxes within your faith.

A paradox is "a statement or proposition that seems self-contradictory or absurd but in reality expresses a possible truth."[8] Without paradoxes, we resist things we don't understand. We resist things we can't control. And we live in an *either/or* world. If you've been alive for twenty-four hours, and you're honest with yourself, you know that we have much more of a *both/and* existence.

Paradoxes tell us that rain can be frustratingly limiting on our day yet beautiful and helpful for our soul. Powdered sugar is messy and leaves the countertops grimy, yet it's delicious and completely necessary to satisfy my sweet tooth. Faith is made up of living in the mystery of the Great Paradox.

Is God with us or in us? Yes

Was Jesus human or divine? Yes.

Does the Bible contain apparent contradictions, but it is entirely true? Yes.

Paradox, by the way, is why I've stayed a Pentecostal. I've always found it the closest to Christian mysticism. A middle ground where experience and education learn to live with mystery. A place where the ethic of love is better than proving which side is right. Some sides were meant to coexist.

One of the greatest paradoxes Jesus reveals is what a person must do to be saved and how they must act afterward. Which pretty much sums up the entirety of the Christian experience. It's easier if we follow the Romans Road, but Christ would rather leave us with an unresolved paradox.

Do you have to "confess with your mouth that Jesus is Lord and believe [it] in your heart" (Romans 10:9, ESV)? Or do you have to sell everything you have and follow Jesus (Matthew 19:21)?

Yes.

What about those prosperity preachers who are constantly making headlines? Shouldn't preachers use their wealth to help the poor and teach others to do the same (Acts 20:35)? Or should we just rejoice that the gospel is being heard, even if it's for selfish gain and false motives (Philippians 1:18)?

Yes.

Are we supposed to stay spiritually hungry to stay blessed (Matthew 5:6)? Or does Jesus satisfy the hunger of all who come to him (John 6:35)?

Yes.

Are we supposed to take up the yoke of Christ and follow him (Matthew 11:29)? Or are we to never submit to a yoke again (Galatians 5:1)?

Yes.

And while we are on the topic of "yokes" in the Bible, why does Jesus say that his yoke is easy in Matthew 11:30, but in Matthew 7:14 he clearly states, "The gateway to life is very narrow and the road is difficult" (NLT)?

Another paradox.

The faith that we rebuild must have a high tolerance for paradoxes if it's going to be built on the words and life of Christ. I haven't even mentioned the paradoxes of just being human. Like the one I am experiencing writing this book: The more I learn, the more I realize how little I know.

Not allowing paradoxes is where we've been colliding with culture. We have used apologetics to corner different worldviews, while those worldviews use the Bible to corner us. It has become a standoff of paradoxical proportions! What if, instead, we believed that mystery is more insightful than certainty, and that following Jesus is highly personal?

4. Make Jesus the unifying doctrine between us and other Christians.

Have you ever wondered why the most cause-oriented generation is so disconnected from the most cause-oriented organization in the world?

I used to plant churches for a living. Starting faith communities is still a passion of mine. Big churches. Small churches. Dinner churches.

All of them offer a fresh expression of the gospel to the world. And while it seems like a good idea, I've always been curious why churches are so quick to post their statements of faith online before they post stories. Churches seem to want people to know what they believe before they show the world who they believe in. We need more stories of how churches are helping heal their communities. I understand that doctrine helps distinguish one church from another, but that's why it's so peculiar. Why are we so focused on distinguishing ourselves from one another? It seems as though Jesus wanted the opposite when he prayed for all of us who believe in him.

> My prayer is not for them alone. I pray also for those who will believe in me through their message, that all of them may be one, Father, just as you are in me and I am in you. May they also be in us so that the world may believe that you have sent me. I have given them the glory that you gave me, that they may be one as we are one—I in them and you in me—so that they may be brought to complete unity. Then the world will know that you sent me and have loved them even as you have loved me.
>
> JOHN 17:20-23

I've heard it said that it's a good thing denominations weren't around when Jesus healed the blind man with mud. Otherwise, we'd have Muddites and Anti-Muddites! It should be no surprise to us that the world doesn't believe there's anything divine about the church when the church refuses to unify around Christ's divinity. When rebuilding, we must let the authority of Jesus be the cornerstone of all fundamentals, distinctives, practices, and traditions. And where we disagree with another's interpretation, we should default to the actions of Jesus. When we don't know what he meant by what he said, can we agree on the reason why he said it? Yes, I'm speaking of that highly debated word: *love*. It seems to be how the world will know that Jesus was sent by God

(1 John 4:9-10). Additionally, it seems to be the unifying action, not belief, that the world will see and recognize that we are sent by God, as well: "Then the world will know that you sent me and have loved them even as you have loved me" (John 17:23).

In every single interview I did with someone who used to be Christian, that person explained they started their exodus from Christianity based on the absence of love. As we rebuild a faith in Jesus, let's remember that if the world doesn't experience God's love, the world won't be transformed by God's love.

When my oldest daughter, Piper, was in kindergarten, my wife and I rotated who made her lunch as we got the kids ready for the day. This time it was my turn, and I had an idea. I started telling my wife about it before fully thinking it through. That's never good!

"Lisa, I have an idea!" I had Piper's empty lunch box in my hand. "I'm not going to pack her lunch today. Instead, I'm going to put an empty lunch box in her backpack. I'll get to her school before her class goes to lunch, and I'll have a bag full of Taco Bell. Quesadillas and cinnamon bites! All her favorites."

"I don't think that's a good idea," Lisa replied. That wasn't the response I was hoping for.

"Why? She'll pull out her empty lunch box as she's turning the corner to the cafeteria and *boom!* I'll be right there to surprise her. Dad of the year!" I didn't anticipate where this could go wrong.

"Preston, what if she goes to her lunch box early for a snack? You know how sad she'll be if she thinks we didn't pack her anything. Pack her a lunch, please."

"Okay. You're right," I conceded. But I didn't do it. I put an empty lunch box in Piper's backpack. *How could this not work?* I thought to myself.

I arrived at the school as planned: fifteen minutes before the kids were dismissed for lunch, with a bag full of Taco Bell in hand. Enough for Piper and all her friends. I could hear her class walking toward me down the hall. There seemed to be a sadness about the conversation. Someone was crying. *Wait . . . I know that cry,* I thought. It was Piper! As soon as I realized it, I heard one of her friends say, "You can have half of my ham sandwich."

Another friend quickly jumped in: "I have graham crackers, if you want one."

Oh, no! Lisa was right. This was a terrible idea. Piper saw an empty lunch box and she was probably hungry. She saw me as she turned the corner. Embarrassed by her empty lunch box, Piper didn't even run to me.

Her teacher was leading the line. "Mr. Ulmer, did you realize you forgot to pack Piper food for the day?" At this point, I ignored her teacher.

"Piper, come here!" I said. She sat in my lap, her cheeks still wet with tears. "Honey, I brought you a whole bag of Taco Bell! I'm sorry that I didn't tell you that. I thought I would surprise you, but instead it was embarrassing." Her expression at this point was somewhere between crying and a smile. I continued, "From now on, if you have an empty lunch box you can rest assured that Dad will be around the corner with a bag full of Taco Bell! More than you will be able to eat. Enough for all your friends."

We hugged tightly. She was finally smiling. I turned to her friends and thanked them for offering her food. "Do you want this instead of a ham sandwich?" I asked one of the generous four-year-olds.

"Yes!" Taco Bell or ham sandwich? There's no competition.

Without our distinctive doctrine, we feel like our lunch box is empty. All the while, the Father is telling us that he has something that unifies us all. Something better than the things we can pack on a website or into a newcomers' class. He has offered us the Bread and Wine. The sacrament that should bring us all together. The night before Jesus died, he prayed what is commonly referred to as the Priestly Prayer. It was a prayer for unity around him. Later, at a table with his disciples, he shared how his body and blood should bring them together. Through his teachings, life, death, and resurrection, we are taught that Jesus is the great meal that we should all share. We shouldn't settle for less. We should strive to empty our lunch boxes. The Father is around the corner!

Who's in the Mountain

When the dust settles, what does the side of the mountain look like now?

Who will people see when they look at your faith?

Do they see your denomination and preferences?

The tenacity of our faith will never change the world. That's left up to the tenacity of our love.

If you are unable to love people how Jesus would love them because of your tribe, it's time to turn in your jersey.

Do they see the Bible when they look at you? That's still not good enough. The Bible tells us stories about God, but it is not the hope of the world. "You study the Scriptures diligently because you think that in them you have eternal life," Jesus said. "These are the very Scriptures that testify about me, yet you refuse to come to me to have life" (John 5:39-40).

Do they see your view of God? We are fighting a losing battle if we think the world needs to think of God just like we do. I'm excited to talk to all the tribes and nations in heaven. I want to hear about their view of God while they were on earth. This doesn't mean God is up for grabs. It just means you haven't cornered the market on God. Faith is a paradox, remember?

Or do they see Jesus? That beautiful picture of God himself who can't be avoided. The One who settled in for thirty-three years to correct all distorted views of religion. The Messiah who audaciously blew up the mountain, replacing the image of Moses and Elijah with his own. The One who the religious have always wanted to crucify. Jesus, the lovely friend of sinners. The One who refused to be twisted by power, no matter how well-intentioned his followers were. He ran from power and into love. Jesus, the reckless lover who willingly entered the jaws of death to convince the world of God's love. Jesus, the One everyone wants to believe in but no one wants to follow.

When people look at your faith, do they see that version of God? The One who entered humanity to declare, "This is who I am. I don't look like that. I look like *this*!"

Perhaps the real question is: What do *you* see when you think of God?

My heart longs to see Jesus when I think of religion, but I'm not there yet. That's why I willingly admit that I'm a deconstructionist. What about you? Can you say that the greatest joy of your life is found in loving the world as Jesus did? Or is the greatest joy of your life telling people about God?

The world doesn't need to hear more of what we believe. They need to see more of who we believe in.

The thought behind this book has been that religion is the mountain. But another thought came to me recently.

What if *we* are the mountain?

What if I'm the obstruction to someone's journey?

What if I'm the immovable object that people are frustrated with?

In which case, the answer is the same—I must still transform into the likeness of Jesus.

Conclusion

A Christianity for Our Kids

"Truth," said a traveller,
"Is a breath, a wind,
A shadow, a phantom;
Long have I pursued it,
But never have I touched
The hem of its garment."

STEPHEN CRANE, *BLACK RIDERS AND OTHER LINES*

The mind that opens to a new idea never returns to its original size.

ALBERT EINSTEIN

IN 2012, A MAN by the name of David Ellis Dickerson was hired by *The American Bible Challenge with Jeff Foxworthy*. His job? "To write exciting, family friendly questions about the Bible." The problem was he wasn't allowed to ask questions that would be offensive or that would contribute to questions about the Bible's coherency. Questions that would spark more questions were out of the picture. As he shared about his time with the show, Dickerson said that these criteria eliminated all but one of the prophets and any questions about the Crucifixion. "People are eating [while they watch this]," he was told. There was a real fear that people's children would be exposed to the Bible.

"So," David said, "we lied. . . . In the process, we sold to our Christian market the kind of wholesome, unified, exciting Bible that they actually believe in. And not the messy, convoluted, fascinating Bible we actually have." Unfortunately, it worked. The debut of that show had the highest-rated views of any show in the history of the gameshow net-work.[1] Americans watched this show without any awareness that behind the scenes, the writers were told to keep it exciting and family friendly. The only problem is that's the exact type of Christianity our family and friends are walking away from.

Writing about people losing their faith is not something that I find enjoyable. The stories in these pages are a lot to process, and I should note that on top of the processing, we will all be reminded of someone (perhaps even yourself) who is on a similar path. May there be a good dosage of grace and spiritual grit given to you as you process these words. Some of my favorite stories to date in life are captured in the vulnerable words of those who live on the fringe. By "fringe," I mean the sacred space of undoing and disassociating with the parts of Christianity that don't line up with a Jesus-looking God. Some Christians think these people live on the edge; I think they are on the verge. My daughter wears a shirt that says, "Kind people are my kind of people." I need to make one that says, "Fringe people are friendly people." Certainly, you know the kind of people I am talking about.

Some have abandoned the church because of the unrealistic nature of "Christian culture." Others have abandoned Christian culture but main-tained an affinity for the church. Some have stopped reading their Bibles due to the subtle (or not-so-subtle) abuses done to them in the name of God. Others consider it their mission to dive deeper into the Bible to restore proper context to the "clobber passages" used against them.

Some cuss. Others barely talk.

Some renounce Christianity. Others are in the middle of reacting against it.

Some want to save Christians. Others want to run from them.

Some fight for more inclusivity. Others don't want to be included.

I don't have any illusions that this book will be a bestseller. If that were what I wanted, I would write a book condemning deconstruction and all of its adherents. Anything that furthers the "us versus them" narrative sells, but I could never do that with a clear conscience. I realize there is nothing about this topic that feels safe or comfortable, especially if you have been part of Christianity for a while. It's easier to stay put, keep your head down, and wait for heaven. I get it.

My hope in writing this wasn't for you to feel comfortable. My hope was for you and me to have a shot at revealing the crucified God to our family and friends. The God who wants more questions, not fewer. The One whose story is chaotic because it's always interwoven in ours. The type of God who can't be contained by traditions or churches. My hope wasn't just for them, though. It's also for you. I don't think *you* are content with the type of Christianity you've been offered.

There is a different way to show up in the world. It's as a worker on the mountain, not a spectator. We each have different tools that will act as dynamite. Mine may be the keyboard of a computer; yours might be a pulpit. Or the break room at work. Or the monotony of everyday parenting. Fill your thoughts with curiosity and your table with curious people. Make it a point to light the FUSE with a few people a year. Bridge the gap in your relationships by earning trust. Lend a listening ear to those who have been hurt. Believe what they say. And help them figure out how to say more.

Don't forget . . .

This is the only way forward.

I fully expect to have to walk through this process with my kids. I expect them to have questions that make me uncomfortable and to draw conclusions that I think are wrong. I expect my sweet daughters to wrestle with grace and truth like I never have. I expect them to dust off my cranky old theology and challenge its usefulness and truthfulness. I expect them to have a more generous orthodoxy than I do. And I expect to repent of things that I feel resolved in today.

Why?

Because I expect to hold my children tighter than my doctrines.

And I imagine you want to do the same.

Acknowledgments

Thank you to everyone who has walked with me as I have gone from a certainty-seeking, dogmatic Christian to a curious Jesus follower. It hasn't been comfortable for so many of you (including me), but your grace, patience, and trust have been the gold streets of heaven along the way. You have led me, supported me, and kept me close.

This book wouldn't be on any shelf if NavPress and Tyndale hadn't decided to get behind it. The NavPress and Tyndale teams work tirelessly at mobilizing the right message. Thank you to David Zimmerman, Olivia Eldredge, Robin Bermel, J. J. Bode, and many more for taking a risk by supporting a book like this. Knowing you supported my research and passion was my saving grace many days. I want to give a special thanks to editors Deborah Gonzalez and Elizabeth Schroll. It's hard to articulate the brilliance behind those two minds. Thank you to my literary agent, Greg Johnson, as well. Greg, you are one of a kind in how you lead authors and live your life.

To my wife, Lisa: Ever since I've known you, you have set the standard for a sharp mind and a compassionate soul. Better than writing a book about Jesus, you read one to our kids every night. And when the interviews in this book made me reconsider much, you held my hands and listened. You are my favorite person!

To my kids, Piper and Brennan: I can trace my curiosity about God back to when you girls were born. I remember thinking that if God loves me half as much as I love you, I have greatly underestimated the love of God. I hope you stay childlike as you discover Jesus as an adult. What a special faith you will find!

To Mom and Dad: You have prayed for years that I would continuously return to the Cross. Now, the authority of the risen Christ is all I want! What God has done in and through your marriage is a testimony that the faith you passed on to me is real. You raised me to ask questions and not settle for anything less than the truth. Thank you for never making me feel like a spiritual misfit in our home. You both are amazing.

To my mother-in-law, Joy: I will find a way to get you into every one of my books! Since Lisa and I have been married, we have changed our minds on many things, but you have never changed your heart toward us. Beyond listening to our stances, you have listened to our stories. May you experience the type of grace you extend to others.

To my pastor, Jeremy Johnson: Do you remember talking about this book while getting a fine breakfast at George's? When I thought I was pushing the envelope too far, you thought I was playing it too safe. Thank you for trusting me with this topic. You are a gift to our family and a force to be reckoned with in the Midwest.

To the Doubters' Club pioneers across the world: You are mobilizing this message more than anyone I have met. You gather the curious to become committed friends through question-based community. I'm so impressed with your faithfulness to everyone who attends. Keep it up!

To the more than sixty-five people I interviewed on this journey: Your stories have fire-branded my soul. I started this book by saying I was venturing into uncharted territory and the fear that surrounded that journey. It is you who made it a safe place. I acknowledge your bravery and care. I hope our lives continue to intertwine past these pages!

To the Church Multiplication Network family: You are truly a family that I hold near and dear to my heart. You have a fierce, optimistic outlook on what this world would look like with more Jesus followers.

To Mike McCrary: You will be surprised to see your name in here (someone text him and tell him). You have never dismissed the message of this book. In fact, you told me to turn it into a dissertation! You called and checked in, shared my angst around this project, and reminded me that people are worth every effort. You're a better friend than you know!

To Josh Hinman, Justin Bryeans, Andy Lehmann, and Jason Bowman: What is there to say about the type of person who is driven by both mission and friendship? I wish the world had more of you. Thank you for always asking me how we are going to get this message further than what I could imagine. I'm very grateful for you.

And finally, I have to acknowledge you—the reader! As I'm writing this acknowledgment, I have no idea how this book made its way into your hands. It took courage for you to continue to turn the pages. Well done! Keep challenging what you think you know for the sake of the person who doesn't know Jesus.

Notes

INTRODUCTION

1. Quoted in John R. W. Stott, *The Cross of Christ*, 20th anniv. ed. (Downers Grove; IVP Books, 2006), 339.
2. Dietrich Bonhoeffer, *God Is in the Manger: Reflections on Advent and Christmas*, trans. O. C. Dean Jr. (Louisville, KY: Westminster John Knox Press, 2010), 22.
3. Bessel van der Kolk, *The Body Keeps the Score: Brain, Mind, and Body in the Healing of Trauma* (New York: Penguin Books, 2014), 17–18.
4. van der Kolk, 18.
5. Melanie Mudge, "What Is Faith Deconstruction?," *Sophia Society* (blog), March 7, 2022, https://www.sophiasociety.org/blog/what-is-faith-deconstruction.
6. Jeffrey M. Jones, "U.S. Church Membership Falls Below Majority for First Time," Gallup, March 29, 2021, https://news.gallup.com/poll/341963/church-membership -falls-below majority-first-time.aspx.
7. John Marriot, *The Anatomy of Deconversion: Keys to a Lifelong Faith in a Culture Abandoning Christianity* (Abilene, TX: Abilene Christian University Press, 2020), 198.

CHAPTER 1 | DECONSTRUCTION IS PART OF OUR SPIRITUAL HERITAGE

1. Upton Sinclair, *I, Candidate for Governor: And How I Got Licked* (Berkeley: University of California Press, 1994), 109.
2. Mark U. Edwards Jr., *Printing, Propaganda, and Martin Luther* (Berkeley: University of California Press, 1994), accessed August 23, 2022, https://publishing.cdlib.org /ucpressebooks/view?docId=ft3q2nb278&chunk.id=d0e303&toc.depth=1&toc.id =d0e303&brand=ucpress. See Table 1, "Totals (Latin + German)" column for cited years.
3. David M. Whitford, "The Papal Antichrist: Martin Luther and the Underappreciated Influence of Lorenzo Valla," *Renaissance Quarterly* 61, no. 1 (Spring 2008): 26–52, https://doi.org/10.1353/ren.2008.0027.

4. "Henry VIII, Martin Luther and Defense of the Seven Sacraments," *A Bit of Henry Love* (blog), accessed August 23, 2022, https://bluffkinghal.wordpress .com/2012/03/13/henry-viii-martin-luther-and-defense-of-the-seven-sacraments/.
5. "The Prophets," BibleProject, YouTube, January 17, 2019, 5:17, https://www .youtube.com/watch?v=edcqUu_BtN0.
6. "The Prophets," BibleProject.

CHAPTER 2 | MORE QUESTIONS THAN ANSWERS

1. The Black Hills—where Mount Rushmore is located—belong to the Lakota people. Their ownership was acknowledged in the 1868 Treaty of Fort Laramie, but this treaty has not been honored by the US government. The Lakota had no say in the conversion of their sacred mountain, Six Grandfathers, into the tourist attraction known as Mount Rushmore. For more on this travesty, see https:// www.doi.gov/blog/mount-rushmore-national-memorial-presidential-tribute; https://www.nationalgeographic.com/travel/article/the-strange-and-controversial -history-of-mount-rushmore; and https://www.youtube.com/watch?v=hX4IvoP1HTk.
2. Dylan Mancy, "75 Surprising Facts about Mount Rushmore," Matador Network, April 21, 2020, https://matadornetwork.com/read75-surprising-facts-mount -rushmore/.
3. Jefferson Bethke, "Why I Hate Religion, But Love Jesus: Spoken Word," Jeff & Alyssa, YouTube, January 10, 2012, 4:03, https://www.youtube.com/watch?v =1IAhDGYlpqY.
4. According to multiple scholars, the book of James was the first divinely inspired epistle written. That would mean James was composed in the middle to late 40s. This may be the reason James never mentions the Jerusalem Council. Perhaps he wrote this letter before the council held any public authority over Jewish Christians. Since the majority (if not all) of James's life was lived in Jerusalem, it would be rather odd for him to have written a letter about Christian action and not mention the council. I'm only defending the early entry of this book into Christian life for one reason. If this is true, then James doesn't just define religion for us.
5. Bethke, "Why I Hate Religion, But Love Jesus."
6. Name has been changed to protect identity.
7. Os Guinness, *Fool's Talk: Recovering the Art of Christian Persuasion* (Downers Grove, IL: IVP Books, 2015), 121.
8. Stephen I. Wright, *Jesus the Storyteller* (Louisville, KY: Westminster John Knox Press, 2015), 9.
9. Henri J. M. Nouwen, *The Return of the Prodigal Son*, anniv. ed. (New York: Convergent, 2016), 21.
10. Nouwen, *Return of the Prodigal*, 48.
11. Tisa Wenger, "Discriminating in the Name of Religion? Segregationists and Slaveholders Did It, Too," *Washington Post*, December 5, 2017, https://www .washingtonpost.com/news/made-by-history/wp/2017/12/05/discriminating -in-the-name-of-religion-segregationists-and-slaveholders-did-it-too/.

12. Nathan McAlone, "Over 68 Million People Watched Documentaries on Netflix in 2016—and It's Helping Them Have a Big Impact," Insider, March 10, 2017, https://www.businessinsider.com/netflix-is-a-documentary-powerhouse -heres-why-2017-3.

13. McAlone, "Over 68 Million People."

CHAPTER 3 | DECONSTRUCTION VERSUS DECONVERSION

1. *Jacques Derrida*, trans. Geoffrey Bennington (Chicago: University of Chicago Press, 1993), 10.

2. For further study on the Emerging Church and why it seems like it was dominated by white males, see https://sojo.net/magazine/may-2010/emerging -church-whites-only?action=magazine.article&issue=soj1005&article =is-the-emerging-church-for-whites-only.

3. Dorothy Day, "In Peace Is My Bitterness Most Bitter," *Catholic Worker* 33, no. 4 (January 1967): 1–2, https://www.catholicworker.org/dorothyday/articles/250.pdf.

4. *Field of Dreams*, directed by Phil Alden Robinson (Universal Pictures, 1989).

5. St. John of the Cross, *The Dark Night of the Soul by St. John of the Cross*, trans. David Lewis (London: Thomas Baker, 1908).

6. Cathy Lynn Grossman, "Christians Drop, 'Nones' Soar in New Religion Portrait," *USA Today*, May 12, 2015, https://www.usatoday.com/story/news/nation/2015 /05/12/christians-drop-nones-soar-in-new-religion-portrait/27159533/.

CHAPTER 4 | DECONSTRUCTION IS ABOUT AUTHORITY

1. María Cecilia Botero as voice of Abuela Alma in *Encanto*, directed by Jared Bush, Byron Howard, and Charise Castro Smith (Walt Disney Animation Studios, 2021), Disney+.

2. John Leguizamo as voice of Bruno in *Encanto*.

3. As quoted in https://drivethruhistory.com/destruction-of-the-temple-foretold-by -jesus/. From Flavius Josephus, *The Wars of the Jews or History of the Destruction of Jerusalem*, Book VII, Chapter 1, paragraph 1.

4. Rabbi Louis Jacobs, "Who Were the Tannaim and the Amoraim?" My Jewish Learning, accessed June 8, 2022, https://www.myjewishlearning.com/article /tannaim-amp-amoraim/.

5. Robert Goldenberg, "Early Rabbinic Explanations of the Destruction of Jerusalem," *Journal of Jewish Studies* 33, no. 1–2 (1982): 517–25.

6. Mike Cosper, "Who Killed Mars Hill?" June 21, 2021, in *The Rise and Fall of Mars Hill*, produced by Mike Cosper, podcast, 56:11, https://www.christianitytoday .com/ct/podcasts/rise-and-fall-of-mars-hill/who-killed-mars-hill-church-mark -driscoll-rise-fall.html.

7. Phyllis Tickle, *The Great Emergence: How Christianity Is Changing and Why* (Grand Rapids, MI: Baker Books, 2008), 16, 19.

8. Name has been changed to protect her privacy.

9. Joseph Conrad, *Victory* (New York: Modern Library, 1921), x–xi.

10. According to the sixty-five interviews I conducted while researching for this book.
11. Philip Yancey, *The Jesus I Never Knew* (Grand Rapids, MI: Zondervan, 1995), 39.
12. Dictionary.com, s.v. "authoritarian (*adj.*)," accessed October 6, 2022, https://www.dictionary.com/browse/authoritarian.

CHAPTER 5 | WWJD? (WHAT WOULD JESUS DECONSTRUCT?)

1. Name has been changed to protect identity.
2. Bart D. Ehrman, *Did Jesus Exist?: The Historical Argument for Jesus of Nazareth* (New York: HarperOne, 2012), chapter 1.
3. These three stances are explained in "Christians & Politics: Where Do You Stand?," ReKnew.org, October 25, 2016, https://reknew.org/2016/10/christians-politics-stand/, adapted from Gregory A. Boyd and Paul Rhodes Eddy, *Across the Spectrum: Understanding Issues in Evangelical Theology* (Grand Rapids: Baker Academic, 2009).
4. "Christians & Politics."
5. "Christians & Politics."
6. Maggie Severns, "In Final Years at Liberty, Falwell Spent Millions on Pro-Trump Causes," *Politico*, December 14, 2020, https://www.politico.com/news/2020/12/14/jerry-falwell-trump-liberty-university-444661.
   Why *did* Jerry Falwell Jr. finally decide to endorse Donald Trump? Michael Cohen, the former attorney (self-described "fixer and designated thug") for President Trump, wrote about this in his book, *Disloyal: A Memoir*. In the book, Cohen talks about the role he played in securing Falwell's vote by promising to protect some racy, personal photographs of the Falwells from becoming public. Years before this, Cohen performed another favor for the Falwells. Jerry wanted to take his daughter to a Justin Bieber concert and asked Cohen for some tickets. Cohen made it happen. Little did Falwell know then that those would be the most expensive Bieber tickets anyone has ever peddled.
   Approaching the 2016 election, there were two substantial favors loaded in Cohen's barrel—Bieber tickets and protecting indecent photos of Jerry and his wife, Becki. "Like the Bieber favor a few years earlier, this would have a huge impact on the 2016 election, evangelicals, the Supreme Court and the fate of the nation," Cohen writes. "In good time, I would call in this favor, not for me, but for the Boss, at a crucial moment on his journey to the presidency."
7. *Fixer and designated thug*: Michael Cohen, *Disloyal: A Memoir: The True Story of the Former Personal Attorney to President Donald J. Trump* (New York: Skyhorse, 2020), foreword. *Like the Bieber favor*: Quoted in Aram Roston, "Trump's Ex-lawyer Cohen Links Falwell's Endorsement in 2016 to Suppression of Racy Photos," Reuters, September 8, 2020, https://www.reuters.com/article/us-usa-falwell-endorsement/trumps-ex-lawyer-cohen-links-falwells-endorsement-in-2016-to-suppression-of-racy-photos-idUSKBN25Z2S0.
8. Robert Costa and Jenna Johnson, "Evangelical Leader Jerry Falwell Jr. Endorses Trump," *Washington Post*, January 26, 2016, https://www.washingtonpost.com/news/post-politics/wp/2016/01/26/evangelical-leader-jerry-falwell-jr-endorses-trump/.

9. Severns, "In Final Years at Liberty."
10. Bradley Onishi, "The Rise of #Exvangelical," Religion & Politics, April 9, 2019, https://religionandpolitics.org/2019/04/09/the-rise-of-exvangelical/.
11. Michael Allen Gillespie, "The Inevitable Entanglement of Religion and Politics," in *Politics, Religion and Political Theology,* ed. C. Allen Speight and Michael Zank (Dordrecht, Netherlands: Springer, 2017), 57.
12. Gregory Boyd, "The Bible, Government and Christian Anarchy," ReKnew.org, January 23, 2008, https://reknew.org/2008/01/the-bible-government-and -christian-anarchy/.
13. Pete Williams, "Supreme Court Stays Out of Ten Commandments Fight," NBC News, updated October 16, 2017, https://www.nbcnews.com/politics/supreme -court/supreme-court-stays-out-ten-commandments-fight-n811071.
14. Linda Kay Klein, *Pure: Inside the Evangelical Movement That Shamed a Generation of Young Women and How I Broke Free* (New York: Atria Paperback, 2018), 13.
15. Definition by Marlene Winell, quoted in Klein, *Pure*, 171.

CHAPTER 6 | F: FIND THE SPECIFICS
1. Christopher Klein, "How Kentucky Became the World's Bourbon Capital," History.com, updated September 1, 2018, https://www.history.com/news/how -kentucky-became-the-worlds-bourbon-capital.
2. David G. Benner, *The Gift of Being Yourself: The Sacred Call to Self-Discovery*, expanded ed. (Downers Grove, IL: IVP Books, 2015), 16.
3. Religion and Ethics Newsweekly, "Sam Harris Extended Interview," November 10, 2006, posted January 5, 2007, https://www.pbs.org/wnet/religionandethics /2007/01/05/january-5-2007-sam-harris-extended-interview/3736/#:~:text=A%3A %20It's%20not%20so%20much,things%20they%20clearly%20cannot%20know.
4. David P. Gushee, *After Evangelicalism: The Path to a New Christianity* (Louisville, KY: Westminster John Knox Press, 2020), 49.
5. Justin Brierley, "Can a Doubter Find a Place in the Church? Preston Ulmer and Gaia McDermott," January 28, 2022, in *Unbelievable?*, podcast, 1:09:57, https:// podcasts.apple.com/us/podcast/can-a-doubter-find-a-place-in-church-preston/ id267242101?i=1000549307465.
6. As quoted (and translated) in Warren W. Wiersbe, *Wiersbe's Expository Outlines on the New Testament* (Colorado Springs: Victor, 1992), 59.
7. For more on David Gushee, see https://davidpgushee.com/about/.
8. Jackson Wu, *One Gospel for All Nations: A Practical Approach to Biblical Contextualization* (Pasadena, CA: William Carey Library, 2015), introduction.

CHAPTER 7 | U: UNDERSTAND WHERE IT CAME FROM
1. Daniel Luzer, "How Lobster Got Fancy," Pacific Standard, updated June 14, 2017, https://psmag.com/economics/how-lobster-got-fancy-59440.
2. Luzer, "How Lobster Got Fancy."
3. Luzer, "How Lobster Got Fancy."
4. Luzer, "How Lobster Got Fancy."

5. Luzer, "How Lobster Got Fancy."

6. Luzer, "How Lobster Got Fancy."

7. Luzer, "How Lobster Got Fancy."

8. Quoted in Luzer, "How Lobster Got Fancy."

9. "Persuasion for the New World: An Interview with Dr. Os Guinness," *Crucible* 4, no. 2 (Summer 1992): 15; quoted in Mark A. Noll, *The Scandal of the Evangelical Mind* (Grand Rapids, Eerdmans, 1994), 23.

10. C. E. B. Cranfield, *The Gospel According to Saint Mark*, Cambridge Greek Testament Commentary series (Cambridge: Cambridge University Press, 1956), 237.

11. Steve Carell as Michael Scott in "Money," *The Office*, season 4, episode 4, originally aired October 18, 2007, on NBC.

12. Stanley Hauerwas, *Resident Aliens: Life in the Christian Colony*, expanded 25th anniv. ed. (Nashville: Abingdon Press, 2014), 85.

13. Paul Arnsberger et al., "A History of the Tax-Exempt Sector: An SOI Perspective," *Statistics of Income Bulletin* (Winter 2008): 105–135, https://www.irs.gov/pub/irs-soi/tehistory.pdf.

14. For a deep dive on such policies, I recommend Kristin Kobes Du Mez, *Jesus and John Wayne: How White Evangelicals Corrupted a Faith and Fractured a Nation* (New York: Liverlight, 2020).

15. Du Mez, *Jesus and John Wayne*, 297–98.

16. Jessica Hugenberg (@welcometotheprocess); https://www.instagram.com/welcometotheprocess/.

17. Quoted in Jean M. Twenge, *iGen: Why Today's Super-Connected Kids Are Growing Up Less Rebellious, More Tolerant, Less Happy—and Completely Unprepared for Adulthood, and What That Means for the Rest of Us* (New York: Atria, 2017), 156.

18. C. S. Lewis, *Out of the Silent Planet* (New York: Scribner, 2003), 56.

CHAPTER 8 | S: SHARE THE IMPACT

1. Dana Arcuri, *Sacred Wandering: Growing Your Faith in the Dark* (self-pub., 2019), 45.

2. I heard this saying from George Harrison, but the original source is: *The Complete Works of Swami Vivekananda, Part I*, 2nd ed. (Mayavati: Prabuddha Bharata Office, 1915), 147.

3. Judith E. Glaser, *Conversational Intelligence: How Great Leaders Build Trust and Get Extraordinary Results* (New York: Bibliomotion, 2014), xxii.

4. Glaser, *Conversational Intelligence*, xiii.

5. Glaser, *Conversational Intelligence*, 8.

6. Glaser, *Conversational Intelligence*, 121–122. "Conversational Dashboard" image copyright © 2014; reproduced by permission of Taylor and Francis Group, LLC, a division of Informa plc.

7. Marco Iacoboni, *Mirroring People: The Science of Empathy and How We Connect with Others* (New York: Picador, 2009).

NOTES

CHAPTER 9 | E: ENGAGE WITH THE REMAINS

1. Quoted in Max Lucado, *In the Eye of the Storm: Jesus Knows How You Feel* (Nashville: Thomas Nelson, 1991), 107–8.
2. "A Conversation with Joan D. Vinge," in Joan D. Vinge, *The Snow Queen*, 35th anniv. ed. (New York: Tor, 2015), 473.
3. Quoted in Bruce Larson, *No Longer Strangers* (Waco, TX: Word Books, 1971), 35–36. Public domain.
4. J. Vernon McGee, *Matthew Chapters 1-13* (Nashville: Thomas Nelson, 1995), 72.
5. G. K. Chesterton, *Orthodoxy* (New York: John Lane Co., 1908), 223.
6. Quoted in Joe Carter, "9 Things You Should Know about G. K. Chesterton," Gospel Coalition, June 14, 2021, https://www.thegospelcoalition.org/article/should-know-chesterton/.
7. Michael Foust, "Skillet's John Cooper: It's Time to 'Declare War' on the Deconstruction Movement," ChristianHeadlines.com, February 10, 2022, https://www.christianheadlines.com/contributors/michael-foust/skillets-john-cooper-its-time-to-declare-war-on-the-deconstruction-movement.html.
8. Dictionary.com, s.v. "paradox (*n.*)," accessed October 6, 2022, https://www.dictionary.com/browse/paradox.

CONCLUSION: A CHRISTIANITY FOR OUR KIDS

1. "Fact checking the Bible: David Ellis Dickerson," TED Archive, YouTube, June 6, 2018, 7:40, https://www.youtube.com/watch?v=7MnCjpw7iBI.

NavPress is the book-publishing arm of The Navigators.

Since 1933, The Navigators has helped people around the world bring hope and purpose to others in college campuses, local churches, workplaces, neighborhoods, and hard-to-reach places all over the world, face-to-face and person-by-person in an approach we call Life-to-Life® discipleship. We have committed together to know Christ, make Him known, and help others do the same.®

Would you like to join this adventure of discipleship and disciplemaking?

- Take a Digital Discipleship Journey at **navigators.org/disciplemaking**.
- Get more discipleship and disciplemaking content at **thedisciplemaker.org**.
- Find your next book, Bible, or discipleship resource at **navpress.com**.

 @NavPressPublishing

 @NavPress

 @navpressbooks

CP1790